The Education of Desire

The Education of Desire

*Towards a Theology
of the Senses*

T. J. Gorringe

The 2000 Diocese of British Columbia
John Albert Hall Lectures
at the
Centre for Studies in Religion and Society
in the University of Victoria

scm press

Copyright © T. J. Gorringe 2001

British Library Cataloguing in Publication Data

A catalogue record for this book is available
from the British Library

0334 02847 7

First published in 2001 by SCM Press
9–17 St Albans Place London N1 0NX

SCM Press is a division of
SCM-Canterbury Press Ltd

Typeset by Regent Typesetting, London
and printed in Great Britain by
Biddles Ltd, Guildford and King's Lynn

for
Bernard

Contents

List of plates

Acknowledgements

1. J. Constable, *Marine Parade and Chain Pier at Brighton*, 1828, oil on canvas, 48½" × 71½" © Tate, London 2001.

2. J. M. W. Turner, *Chain Pier at Brighton*, 1828, oil on canvas, 71 × 136.5 cm. © Tate, London 2001.

3. F. Bacon, *Portrait of Isabel Rawsthorne*, 1966, oil on canvas, 26¾" × 8⅛". © Estate of Francis Bacon/ARS, NY and DACS, London 2001.

4. Rembrandt van Rijn, *Self-Portrait Aged 63*, c. 1665, oil on canvas, 114.3 × 94 cm. Reproduced by courtesy of the Trustees, The National Gallery, London.

5. Velazquez, *Innocent X*, 1650, oil on canvas, 78 × 68 cm. Reproduced with permission of Galleria Doria-Pamphili, Rome.

6. Caravaggio, *John the Baptist*, c. 1603–5, oil on canvas, 172.5 × 104.5 cm. Reproduced by permission of The Nelson-Atkins Museum of Art, Kansas City, Missouri (Purchase: Nelson Trust) 52-25, photography by Robert Newcombe and Edward Robinson.

7. G. Grosz, *The Painter of the Hole*, 1947–8, 89.6 × 69.3 cm. Reproduced by courtesy of the Busch-Reisinger Museum, Harvard University Art Museums, Association Fund.

Preface

The first four chapters of this book are an annotated version of the John Albert Hall lectures given at the University of Victoria, British Columbia, in September 2000 under the title 'In the realm of the senses'. I have changed the title for the published version because I need to signal how fragmentary these attempts at a theology of the senses are. The fifth chapter is a version of a lecture given to the Catholic Peace and Justice Conference in July of the same year, and then to the clergy in North and South Vancouver Island. It develops themes which were only alluded to in the fourth lecture, but the difference in style will be obvious.

I have to thank Michael Hadlee above all for the invitation to come to Victoria. It was his interest in my work on criminal justice which was responsible for the invitation in the first place. He and his wife, Anita, were extremely generous, gracious and tactful hosts. Harold Coward, Director of the Centre for Studies in Religion and Society, which organizes the lectures, proved a stimulating, rigorous and challenging dialogue partner, drawing on a range of expertise which far exceeds my own. He and Rachel, his wife, were likewise extremely gracious hosts.

There were many other sources of stimulus in Vancouver Island, amongst whom I would like particularly to mention Greg Shoop, Sonia Furstenau, John Wright and the members of the William Head Penal Institution Restorative Justice Circle. Long may they continue to discuss Hannah Arendt!

In Exeter I would like to thank my colleague Jeremy Law, always generous with his time, who has provided valuable critical comment on two of the chapters. It is a great pleasure to have such a committed theologian to work with.

The book is dedicated to a great Anglican Franciscan, Bernard, who over a lifetime has educated the desire of countless people in Britain, Australia and elsewhere, and who has lived out that affirmative, body-welcoming asceticism which seems to me a crucial factor in tackling that environmental crisis which, for the foreseeable future, is going to be the key ethical issue we all face.

Tim Gorringe
Exeter
All Saints Day 2000

Instruments of grace

What significance do the senses have for our theological understanding? By way of beginning to reflect on that question I want to consider two images of Brighton pier, painted in the early decades of the nineteenth century. The first is that of Constable (1776–1837), the second of Turner (1775–1851).

Although Constable painted very few conventionally religious pictures, he was a deeply religious painter. 'Who', he asked in his *Landscape Scenery*, 'in the ardour of youth, would not willingly forgo the vainer pleasures of society, and seek his reward in the delights resulting from the love and study of Nature, and in his successful attempts to imitate her in the features of the scenery with which he is surrounded; so that in whatever spot he may be placed, he shall be impressed with the beauty and majesty of Nature under all her appearances, and thus be led to adore the hand that has, with such lavish beneficence, scattered the principles of enjoyment and happiness through every department of Creation.'[1] This was no isolated pious sentiment. In the last of his lectures on landscape painting in 1835, he wrote, 'The landscape painter must walk in the fields with a humble mind. No arrogant man was ever permitted to see nature in all her beauty. If I may be allowed to use a very solemn quotation, I would say most emphatically to the student, 'Remember now the Creator in the days of thy youth . . . the art of seeing nature is a thing almost as much to be acquired as the art of reading the Egyptian hieroglyphics.'[2] Constable is, and sought to be, a painter of creation. He is the painter of Genesis 1. If we wanted an epigraph for his work it would be: 'And God saw all that God had made and behold it was very good.' We see it in his account of the Chain pier, painted in 1827 (Plate 1). His back is to the sun, as usual, as when one takes a photograph, allowing the greatest depth for light and shade. Chiaroscuro, in fact, was his passion from first to last. His cloudscapes are justly celebrated. They are not just imaginative background material but profoundly accurate. Constable's father intended him to take over the family mill, and he trained for that for a while. As such he had to understand the weather in order to set the sails appropriately. In this picture we see a sou'wester blowing up from the channel, the clouds massing, and a stiff breeze keeling the little fishing boats offshore. In half an hour it will be pouring with rain.

Turner, born a year after Constable, was almost his opposite. Where Constable was uxorious, he never married; where Constable had to wait nearly thirty years for membership of the Royal Academy, Turner was admitted at 22; where Constable was born a gentleman, Turner was the son of a barber; where Constable left us vivid and tender correspondence, Turner liked to keep his counsel. He is not known to have been overtly religious, and like Constable rarely painted religious scenes. But theologically we can see that he was an eschatological painter. He is the painter of the book of Revelation. He always paints *into* the sun, not with his back to it. He paints the world irradiated with glory, and this vision grew stronger with every year of his life. His epigraph is from Ezekiel: 'And there, the glory of the God of Israel was coming from the east . . . and the earth shone with his glory' (Ezek. 43.2). As so often in his paintings, his theme is more light than it is the pier, which threatens to evaporate (Plate 2).

Art is a school of attention and, as Simone Weil put it, prayer consists in attention. All great art helps us to see, attend to, sense, the depth, mystery and glory of God's creation. This is especially true of the great landscape painters of the beginning of the nineteenth century. In the light of their work let us pose the question, 'Why a world?' Why this material sensual place, this interweaving of quarks and gluons, which we inhabit? Why blood, bone, semen and faeces? Why senses?

Of course there is a standard theological answer: to constitute a vale of soul-making. For the emergence of free and loving creatures we need the kind of world we inhabit. I think that answer, properly nuanced, cannot be dispensed with, and I shall be reflecting on it in the second chapter, but it is not what I want to begin with. The emphasis falls on pain, suffering and evil. But we read in John's prologue:

> And the word became *flesh*, and we beheld his *glory*. (John 1.14)

Flesh (matter, the material) is patent of glory. In applying to Jesus of Nazareth it applies to humanity, and indeed to matter as a whole, as the patristic Christology always insisted. This is part of what it means to say that God saw all that God had made, and behold, it was very good.

Another, more orthodox, suggestion is that the purpose of the whole of creation was the incarnation, God's taking flesh in Christ. In Karl Barth's words: 'The reason why God created this world of heaven and earth, and why the future world will be a new heaven and a new earth . . . is that God's eternal Son and Logos did not will to be an angel or animal but a man, and that this and this alone was the content of the eternal divine election of grace.'[3] Distinguished as the advocates of this view are, it again does not do justice to creation in both its grandeur and its tragedy.

Another suggestion, with a gnostic, or perhaps Hegelian, pedigree, is that 'God came down into the world as into a mirror. He came down in order to possess an image of his own divinity. And he will allow man to be "saved", in order to save that fragment of his image captured in the divine soul.'[4] This is a completely narcissistic idea of God, but it articulates the idea that God has God's own purposes in and for creation and on this idea I want to build.

At the heart of a theology of the senses is the perception that the possibilities of the material lie within the immaterial God, that the material is not foreign to God, but a form of God's self-expression. Christianity has always rejected the Manichaean option that creation was a mistake. If creation was from nothing, then creation represented a choice, an option for matter. To the argument that such a world was necessary for beings who could learn to love freely, a focus on the senses adds the dimensions of beauty and of exploration. If the creation is patent of glory then the senses, material themselves, are what allow us to explore that. The senses are what allow us to explore the world we are given, but I want to go further and suggest God chooses this form of reality, and endows us with senses, to celebrate and to explore the mystery and the magic of God's own creation. Not just that we celebrate and explore it, but that God celebrates and explores through us.

God celebrates. What was God's purpose in creating human beings? The answer of the Heidelberg Catechism is: 'To love him and glorify him for ever' (Qu. 6). Humans celebrate their creator. But according to Scripture it is the other way about as well: God celebrates this gracious creation, and us within it. There is the fine text of Zephaniah 3.17:

> The Lord your God is in your midst, a warrior who gives victory; he will rejoice over you with gladness, he will renew you in his love; he will joy (*gil*) over you with loud singing as on a day of festival.

The verb translated joy or exult means to leap or dance. What the text actually says is that God dances over us, dances with joy over God's creation, celebrates in song and dance.

What does God celebrate? Consider the famous text of Hosea:

> It was I who taught Ephraim to walk,
> I took them up in my arms . . .
> I was to them like those who lift infants to their cheeks.
> I bent down and fed them. (Hos. 11.4)

The text images God as the fond parent, teaching God's child to walk. Parents celebrate their children's achievements, no matter how ordinary or inadequate, by any objective standard, they may be. When our children excel we are more thrilled than they are. I want to suggest that God celebrates the achievements of the creature. The answer to the question 'Why a world?' is not just that the creature can glorify God, but that God can rejoice in the creature, and what the creature achieves. This is, I think, consistent with the image of the loving parent which we find in the parables of Jesus. It is not just a question of concern for our welfare, for our wrong or right doing, but for what we do with our gifts. What we do with the talents given us is not, according to the parable, a purely incidental matter.

The English poet Elizabeth Jennings has said that Freud was a worse disaster in the twentieth century than Hitler and Stalin. But we can never be too grateful to Freud for highlighting for us the way in which we replace the God of the gospel with the domineering God of the super-ego. That God does not exist. He is a nightmare projection. The true God is not in competition with us and does not seek our subjugation. Moreover the freedom God gifts us is true freedom, a portion of God's own. This is why, as in the talents parable (Matt.

25.15 ff.), God waits to see what we will do with it, and what good things will come from it, and this is a large part of what we mean by grace. Grace is radical giftedness. It is God's existence as the gifting One in the first place, but it is also the character of what God gifts to us, not only free, as every gift is, but also grace-ful – true, holy, good and beautiful.

So far so good. To say that God celebrates the creature has scriptural warrant and may seem relatively uncontentious. But what about the suggestion that God explores the creation through the creature? What sense does it make to say that of an infinite, omniscient and omnipresent being? In her profound study, *The Body in Pain*, Elaine Scarry argues that in the Hebrew Bible God makes God's reality known by what she calls scenes of wounding: the toil attached to labour, the pains of childbirth, the flood, plagues, fire and brimstone, leprous sores, and so on and so forth. 'However more powerful the Word of God is than the Body of man, it is within these stories always the case that the Word is never self-substantiating: it seeks its confirmation in a visible change in the realm of matter.'[5]

> Throughout the writings of the patriarchs and the prophets, we again and again and again return to a scene of wounding. It is a scene that carries emphatic assurance about the 'realness' of God . . . The powerful God does not have the power of self substantiation. The body is not simply an element in a scene of confirmation; it *is* the confirmation. Apart from the human body, God himself has no material reality except for the countless weapons that he exists on the invisible and disembodied side of.[6]

Scarry is assuming, with the bulk of the Judaeo-Christian tradition, that God has no body and that God therefore uses the body of the creature as it were vicariously. But does God have a body? The deist theologians were prepared to speak of the created universe as God's sensorium. Recently both Grace Jantzen and Sally McFague have argued that we need to think of the universe as God's body.[7] The problem with denying God a body is, of course, that we have no idea how one can be a person without a body, and whatever else we want to say of God we want to say that God is personal, that we can cry 'Abba, Father' to God, and speak as an I to a Thou. Denying God a body seems to commit us to a resolute soul–body dualism, the argument that persons are properly souls and that bodies are merely contingent, a consequence that Richard Swinburne, for example, is perfectly prepared to draw.[8] This is a minority option today partly because of our understanding of the scriptural view of the human, which is clearly of a body–soul unity, and partly because the human sciences also point strongly away from such dualism. Precisely on these grounds Jantzen wants to think of the universe as God's body, but here too there are formidable difficulties. Pantheism compromises divine transcendence. Jantzen argues that God transcends the universe as the soul, or human agency, transcends the body, so that God cannot be reduced to the processes of creation.[9] It would be open to the objector, however, to point to the limitations the body imposes on the soul. To some extent we are what our bodies allow us, or teach us, to be. Looking at the created order Hume said he was led to think most of the 'slow rotting of a turnip' – not the most encouraging image for transcendence. There are worse difficulties. Jantzen acknowledges, but to my mind does not sufficiently answer, the problem that the identification of the universe with God's body writes evil and suffering into the very essence of God. We can say that the model teaches us that God, too, suffers, but then the question of agency arises. Jantzen is right to point out that both here, and in the question of determinism, classical theism is equally vulnerable, but it certainly has the merit of depicting God as agent much more emphatically. The model also inevitably downplays the gap between creator and creature, suggesting that the creature shares in the divine in a stronger sense than Christianity has ever wanted to affirm. The doctrine of creation *ex nihilo* not only maintains the divine freedom, but underlines the fact that the creature is in no sense divine. Furthermore, I cannot see that the proposal of either of these authors has any advantage over the traditional understanding of divine immanence which, in Barth's construal of it at least, is not about some quasi-material presence everywhere, but about God's infinitely differentiated and personal presence not *in* but *to* the creation.[10] This is especially true for McFague, who wants to emphasize the metaphorical nature of her proposal. If we are going to change the metaphors there must be real advantages in doing so, and that is not clear here. It seems to me, there-fore, that there are good reasons for going with the tradition and refusing to speak of the universe as God's body. In that case, Scarry implies, God experiences the bodily through us.

Of course Christianity has always wanted to say that in the incarnation God assumed a body, which knew hunger, thirst and presumably puberty and the stirring of desire, as well as pain and death. There is, as Scarry puts it, a profound change in the state of the religious imagination in the New Testament. Where, in the Hebrew Bible, God's reality is known through human wounding, in the New Testament it is God who is wounded. 'The sentient body of God is touched by the sentient body of man.'[11] But does the incarnation change, once for all, the structure of the divine relation to creation? Does the divine assumption of body render otiose the vicarious relation to the human body we find in the Hebrew Bible? I do not think it does, and the reason for so thinking rests with the assumption of the relation of the free creature to the free God. Clearly God did not create a puppet theatre – that would make no sense of the gospel story. Neither did God make a shadow theatre, on the lines of Plato's allegory of the cave. Perhaps the image of the theatre is really off track, venerable and suggestive as it is, for the One who loves in freedom created those who could love in freedom in return. The One who creates in the inexhaustibility of divine imagination gifts imagination to the creature. The One who is the source of all beauty allows beauty to be explored. As a number of theologians have argued over the past fifty years, I think we have to distance ourselves from the God of classical theism who knows everything in one infinite and eternal act of knowledge. I understand the logic which leads to the position, but the God it ends up with really seems to me a prisoner of his own attributes. God really loves in freedom, which means the freedom of self-limitation, of joy in the creature's discoveries. Human creativity ranges and explores the mystery of God's creation. And this exploration and creating is God's delight, the cause of the exultation Zephaniah speaks of.

For the exercise of this freedom God chooses embodiment, and not just in Christ. God chooses materiality in the first place, according to Genesis. That is God's option. This is counterintuitive to the Greek tradition. The philosopher, says Socrates in *Phaedo*, frees himself as far as possible from the body. The soul reflects best when it is free from the distraction of the senses. In fact it despises the body.[12]

For the Christian, on the other hand, salvation is bodily. It is accomplished by the body of Christ, into which our bodies are incorporated. As Eugene Rogers puts it, 'For Christians, bodies are no more or less than a means by which God catches hold of and sanctifies human beings. In short, bodies are made to be saved. Union with God does not take place otherwise than by incorporating their physical bodies into God's.'[13]

And bodies mean senses. We can see from the *Confessions* that Augustine was a natural aesthete who gloried in all the senses. At one point in his life, however, he was touched by what Peter Brown speaks of as a kind of wild Platonism.[14] For this reason he went back to another Christian Platonist, Origen, and spoke of five *spiritual* senses.

> When I love you, what do I love? It is not physical beauty nor temporal glory nor the brightness of light dear to earthly eyes, nor the sweet melodies of all kinds of songs, nor the gentle odour of flowers and ointments and perfumes, nor manna or honey, nor limbs welcoming the embraces of the flesh; it is not these I love when I love my God. Yet there is a light I love, and a food, and a kind of embrace when I love my God – a light, voice, odour, food, embrace of my inner man, where my soul is floodlit by light which space cannot contain, where there is a sound that time cannot seize, where there is a perfume which no breeze disperses, where there is a taste for food no amount of eating can lessen, and where there is a bond of union that no satiety can part. That is what I love when I love my God.[15]

It is beautiful, but it is not the gospel. Here it seems to me that Karl Marx was much nearer the truth when he wrote, as a young man, that: 'Humankind is affirmed in the objective world not only in the act of thinking but with all their senses. The forming of the five senses is a labour of the entire history of the world down to the present.'[16] The Christian will add: and that is part of the divine intention. Aquinas was quite sure that in heaven all our senses, with the possible exception of taste, would be at their greatest perfection, and fully active. In heaven, as on earth, the senses 'conduce to the integrity of human nature and show forth the wisdom of their Creator'.[17] The senses are the means through which we explore materiality, or rather, I am suggesting, *the means by which God chooses to explore materiality through us*, just as the Spirit prays through us, according to Paul (Rom. 8.26). Paul's text suggests that precisely as beings who live through our senses we live within that Trinitarian pattern of relationship in which is grounded the possibility of matter. As the created universe stems from, and to some extent reflects, that divine relationality, so the Spirit guides, works with, celebrates through, the responsive creature's exploration of creation.

This is not to suggest that God is dependent on the creature to know creation, which would be absurd. But precisely because God is Wholly Other, absolutely transcendent, the creator of all that is, God can choose to see what will come of the senses in terms of music, art, all the exercise of the imagination. Naturally we think at once of the great artists, of Bach and Mozart or of Leonardo and Botticelli, but in this exploring I want to emphasize the sensual life in all its everydayness, as Jesus does in his parables. To turn to the image of the loving parent once again, so prominent in Scripture, none of us thinks a whit less of our children if they do not turn out a genius. In small ways the life of each of us is the exercise of creativity in which God delights, and we are expected to use our gifts as the parable of the talents makes clear. We exercise our creativity through our senses. God saw all that God had made, and it was very good. That 'good' in a material world involves colour, texture, tonality, density, aroma, taste. We explore it through our senses. The senses are what are given us to know what 'grace' means, to explore, as the author of Ephesians puts it, the breadth, length, height and depth of the love of God manifest in creation (Eph. 3.18). 'We declare to you what was from the beginning, what we have heard, what we have seen with our eyes, and what we have looked at and touched with our hands, concerning the word of life . . . we declare to you what we have seen and heard so that you also may have fellowship with us' (1 John 1.1–3). The author speaks of the incarnate Word, but I want to argue that this applies more broadly to the whole creation God has gifted us. Senses, I want to say, are a gift of God, are grace, part of that radical imaginative gifting of God. We respond in gratitude by using them, and in so doing the Spirit prays, knows and celebrates through us.

This implies no aestheticization of existence. Speaking of the need to come to terms with AIDS, Vereene Parnell talks of the 'absolute necessity of taking the physicality of human life seriously and the unqualified obscenity of all attempts to romanticize that corpo-reality'.[18] As she worked with congregations committed to helping those with AIDS she noted that 'Colours, sounds and smells establish resonances within our own bodies, but corporeality embraces a different intimacy as well. Repeatedly, my partners in this project brought me back to the flesh on flesh experience of incarnation, an embodied encounter requiring an embodied response.'[19] The affirmation and celebration of the senses is clearly here, as it must be in incarnational faith, part and parcel of the living out of ethics.

At this point I must anticipate some immediate objections, and in so doing sketch out the course of this book. If you are going to put so much weight on the senses, you can object, what about those who are sensually deprived, those who are not just partially sighted but completely blind; those who are profoundly deaf; those who are quadraplegic? It is an important question, and I take it up in the second chapter. Or, you can say, fine to celebrate the senses, but they are used for evil as well as for good. Of course. And I turn to that question in the third chapter. And then, aren't the senses the basis of our present hedonist, consumerist society, and if so, aren't you affirming that? And where does the ancient theme of Christian asceticism fit in your scheme? That is the theme of the fourth chapter. Finally I turn to the sacramental affirmation of the body which is the central act of worship of the Christian community, the eucharist.

Let me turn now to the senses as gift. I am going to go through them one by one, but of course they can only notionally be distinguished. 'The senses translate each other without any need of an interpreter', says Merleau-Ponty, 'and are mutually comprehensible without the intervention of any idea.'[20] Perhaps that is to put it too simply, for of course it is accumulated memory, beginning at birth, which teaches us to make sense of the world.[21] The human infant both constructs a world through the senses and is given a world through her or his culture, as the social anthropologists have taught us.

The senses give us our world, and they do so together. Nevertheless, from at least the time of Plato, up to the present, there has been a competition for which is the most important of the senses, and there is a general consensus that Greece prioritized sight whilst Israel prioritized hearing. In more recent times an argument has been made for the supremacy of touch. Taste and smell have always come rather low down the list, but most of us would prefer not to imagine a world without them. In view of the mutual imbrication of the senses I prefer not to play this game. Since I have to start somewhere, however, and since as a theologian I work within the Judaeo-Christian tradition, I am going to begin with hearing.

Hearing

'In the beginning was the Word.' Mountains of exegesis attend the opening of John's Gospel, looking at Greek and Hermetic sources, but without doubt the primary source is the Hebrew Bible, where no less than 93% of the uses of *dabar* YHWH refer to a prophetic word. Through this word the prophet is set 'over nations and over kingdoms, to pluck up and to pull down, to destroy and to overthrow' (Jer. 1.10).

The priority of the oral over the visual in human cultures is linked to the lateness of the discovery and distribution of writing. That the Hebrew Bible comes from a predominantly oral culture may have something to do with the predominance of the Word in both Old and New Testaments, but I suspect there are still more fundamental reasons, two of which are highlighted by Walter Ong's great study, *The Presence of the Word*. The first is that the word of a person marks their *interiority*. 'Because the spoken word moves from interior to interior, encounter between man and man is achieved largely through voice . . . Encounters with others in which no words are ever exchanged are hardly encounters at all.'[22] The film *Last Tango in Paris*, in which the main protagonists only grunt at one another for most of the action, and which ends with alienation and death, illustrates this perfectly. 'Voice', says Ong, 'for man the paradigm of all sound, manifests the actual use of power by the most interior of interiors, a person. In a universe conceived in terms of auditory synthesis, the sense of personal activity is overwhelming.'[23] It is for this reason that, without help, the congenitally deaf are far more intellectually retarded than the congenitally blind, as Aristotle already pointed out.[24] The word as interior corresponds to a world of depth. Ong likes to quote Eugen Rosentock-Huessy's remark that experiences of the first order, of the first rank, are never realized through the eye. 'The world of sound has proved in all cultures the most immediate sensory coefficient of thought. Sight may provide a great deal of the material to think about, but the terms in which all men do their thinking correspond to words, that is to sounds.'[25] To come down from this high level for a moment, I like the remark of Isabel Allende that women's sensuality is tied to the imagination and the auditory nerves. 'The G spot is in the ear,' she says, 'and if anyone goofs about looking for it any further down they are wasting their time and ours.'[26]

Let us ask what this interiority would mean in terms of the idea of God exploring God's creation through the creature. It has echoes of divine immanence, the idea that God is closer to the creature than the creature itself. But it also says something, I think, about the graciousness of God's presence. Of course, the Word can be compelling as it was for Jeremiah, for whom it became 'like a burning fire, pent up in my bones', but characteristically it was a 'still, small voice', and not a shout or a stentorian command. This has usually been taken to be the voice of conscience or of reason, but is it not, as Proverbs represents it, the voice of invitation (Prov. 9)?

A second point about the Word is that it is a land bounded on all sides. 'It is decisively the fact that language does have its frontiers', says George Steiner, 'that it borders on three other modes of statement – light, music and silence – that gives proof of a transcendent presence in the fabric of the world. It is just because we can go no further, because speech so marvellously fails us, that we experience the certitude of a divine meaning surpassing and enfolding ours. What lies beyond man's word is eloquent of God. That is the joyously defeated recognition expressed in the poems of St John of the Cross and of the mystic tradition. Where the word of the poet ceases, a great light begins.'[27] As we know, silence may often be more profoundly communicative than words, though it needs to be defined by them.

If language is bounded on one side by silence, on another side there is music. Despite the overwhelming emphasis on hearing in Scripture there is very little reflection on music, except for Psalm 150's encomium on the Temple jazz band. By contrast Plato was deeply exercised by music, and in a move he was sure would appeal to all right thinking people wanted to ban the Spice Girls, Britney Spears and Boyzone from the Republic. One of the reasons for this is that he regarded songs as 'spells for the soul'.[28] There are clearly good spells and bad spells. Musical education held a key place in his scheme of things because 'more than anything else rhythm and harmony find their way to the inmost soul and take strongest hold upon it, bringing with them and imparting grace, if one is rightly trained, and otherwise the contrary . . . omissions and the failure of beauty in things badly made or grown would be more quickly perceived by one who was properly educated in music and so, feeling distaste rightly, he would praise beautiful things and take delight in them and receive them into his soul to foster its growth and become himself beautiful and good.'[29] Aristotle also includes a place for music in the *Politics*. It may, he says, 'be pleasurable and refresh the mind; it may present moods such as anger, calm, fortitude, temperance or release emotions or stimulate to action; or it may be an object of speculative inquiry, making a contribution to the cultivation of our minds and the growth of moral wisdom.'[30] His distinctions correspond to later formalist, expressivist, metaphysical and ethical accounts of music. In particular on the part of the poets there has been, says Steiner, a recurrent acknowledgement that 'music is the deeper, more numinous code, that language, when truly apprehended, aspires to the condition of music and is brought, by the genius of the poet, to the threshold of that condition'.[31] And the theological question is this: what does the power of music have to say to us about the God who is the origin of all its possibilities? It is God who is the origin of music's power to express emotion, to lead us to dance, to reduce us to tears. All this has its origin in God, and we explore the depths of God's world and of its imaginative possibilities in making music. Barth famously said that the music of Mozart caused us to hear the peace past understanding in creation, but there is joy and tragedy to hear as well, stemming from the depths of God's imagination.

Sight

I move now from hearing to sight. For some centuries, it is said, we have lived in a culture which privileges sight over all the other senses, a fact which some trace to the rediscovery of perspective at the end of the fifteenth century, or to the development of printing by Johannes Gutenberg in 1454. In fact, acknowledgement of the primacy of sight goes back to ancient times. Although in the *Phaedrus* Plato was inclined to privilege hearing, in the *Timaeus* he described vision as humanity's greatest gift.[32] According to Aristotle sight is 'in its own right the superior sense' because, thanks to the fact that all things are coloured, it 'brings tidings of multitudes of distinctive qualities of all sorts; whence it is through this sense especially that we perceive the common sensibles, viz figure, magnitude, motion, number'.[33] Francis Bacon at the beginning of the sixteenth century would 'admit nothing but on the faith of the eyes'.[34] A couple of decades later Descartes agreed: 'All the management of our lives depends on the senses, and since that of sight is the most comprehensive and the noblest of these, there is no doubt that the inventions which serve to augment its power are among the most useful that there can be.'[35]

There is good neurological reason for this view. In terms of neural equipment the eye is far superior to the other senses.

Having some 18 times more nerve endings than the cochlear nerve of the ear, its nearest competitor, the optic nerve with its 800,000 fibres is able to transfer an astonishing amount of information to the brain, and at a rate of assimilation far greater than that of any other sense organ. In each eye, over 120 million rods take in information on some 500 levels of lightness and darkness, while more than 7 million cones allow us to distinguish among more than one million combinations of colour. The eye is also able to accomplish its tasks at a far greater remove than any other sense, hearing and smell being only a distant second and third.[36]

This capacity of the eye means that more than any of the other senses it is responsible for giving us our world. 'The eye accomplishes the prodigious work of opening the soul to what is not soul – the joyous realm of things and their god, the sun . . . Vision encounters, as at a crossroads, all the aspects of Being.'[37] We recognize this in our everyday speech. We say: Seeing is believing; I couldn't believe my eyes, and so on. But we are also frequently told that vision is a dissecting, objectifying and distancing sense, and we consider one way in which this is true in the third chapter, but it is not the whole story. For the medieval mind, light was the most direct manifestation of God. 'According to the Platonizing metaphysic of the Middle Ages,' writes Otto von Simson, 'light is the most noble of natural phenomena, the least material, the closest approximation to pure form.

> At the basis of all medieval thought is the concept of analogy . . . The degree to which a thing 'resembles' God, to which God is present in it, determines its place in the hierarchy of beings . . . We understand a piece of wood or a stone only when we perceive God in it, a medieval writer observes. Hence the connection between the 'aesthetics of light' and the 'metaphysics of light' in the middle ages . . . In the physical light that illuminated the sanctuary, that mystical reality seemed to become palpable to the senses.[38]

The medieval cathedrals, von Simson is saying, were built to instantiate and make possible the metaphysics of light the theologians believed in. He believes that experience is closed to us. But is it? Here is the novelist Rosemary Sutcliff, a victim of Still's disease, writing of a period of her life when she was both loved and in love. The year is 1947, and in Britain it was the worst winter of the twentieth century. The thaw was a long time coming. Then, suddenly, at the end of March,

> The narrow high-walled garden of Daniel's Cottage was flickering with the coloured flame points of crocuses, white and purple and lilac and gold, and each crocus opening to the sunlight seemed to me at once a star and a grail; a cup brimming with light. It is one of the Mysteries, surely, this sense of light shining *through* rather than *on*; the whole world becoming faintly translucent and the light of the spirit shining through its substance, that comes with being in love.[39]

What the medieval theologians and builders sensed, and what Rosemary Sutcliff is sensing – and I use the word advisedly – is the sheer gracious beauty of the world which mirrors the gracious beauty of God in Godself. This, too, is what Turner saw. Turner 'seems to paint with tinted steam' said Constable of two 1836 paintings, 'so evanescent and airy'. He demonstrates, says Ronald Paulson, that landscape can be essentially about light as we see more and more in his later paintings, and especially those of Venice.[40] These paintings, and especially his 1843 *Light and Colour*, or *The Morning After the Deluge*, both understand the created world in terms of light, and recall Ezekiel's whirlwind, with 'a fire infolding itself, and a brightness . . . about it, and out of the midst thereof as the colour of amber, out of the midst of the fire' (Ezek. 1.4).[41]

Touch

I move on now to touch. Some have claimed that touch remained the master sense until at least the eighteenth century, and that it tests and confirms what sight could only perceive.[42] In Aristotle we find the surprising remark that, 'While in respect of all the other senses we fall below many species of animals, in respect of touch we far excel all other species in exactness of discrimination. That is why man is the most intelligent of animals. This is confirmed by the fact that it is to differences in the organ of touch and to nothing else that the differences between man and man in respect of natural endowment are due; men whose flesh is hard are ill endowed with intellect, men whose flesh is soft, well endowed.'[43] Touch here obviously endorses the old idea of the aristocracy as those who do no hand labour.

Theologically the most significant dimension of touch, as both Emmanuel Levinas and, following him, Enrique Dussel have realized, is the caress. If we are lucky, and we are a wanted child, then caresses and cuddles are our first experience of touch, grounding our sense of security and self-worth for the rest of our lives. If the Christian story is true, and this is how artists have depicted it through the ages, then Christ knew this himself. Of course it doesn't last. As H. G. Wells put it in *Mr Polly*:

> There had been a time when two people had thought Mr Polly the most wonderful and adorable thing in the world, and kissed his toe-nails, saying 'myum myum!' and marvelled at the exquisite softness and delicacy of his hair, had called to one another to remark the peculiar distinction with which he bubbled . . . and wrapped him up in soft warm blankets and smothered him with kisses.

By the time he was thirteen, however, his father, 'who had long since forgotten the time when his son's little limbs seemed to have come straight from the hand of God . . . remarked – "It's time that dratted boy did something for a living." ' Well, that's life. Never mind, again if we are lucky we are able both to receive and to bestow the caresses of a lover. 'Sexual intention', says Dussel, 'begins by touch, contact, caress. Caressing is nearness, proximity; it is a progression restrained by modesty but tempted by profanation, in which two persons advance and draw back, asking the other as other, without words, whether their desires are mutual.' In some feminist writing, especially that of Andrea Dworkin, it is assumed that sexual intercourse between a man and a woman is always about invasion, penetration, violence. It seems men are ontological rapists. I want to ask – is it not, when it is an experience of love, actually a form of caress? Dussel again: 'Coitus is one of the privileged metaphysical experiences of the human being. It is access to the area of reality beyond the horizon of the world. It is beyond reason, where desire takes us as a satisfaction of the other's desire . . . The sexual organ is in the human being the presence in totality of the absence of the other; it is a call to the realization of the other in the other's negativity.'[44]

Perhaps that again doesn't last, and *Mr Polly* illustrates that too, but touch does not cease to be important. We all know the touch of affirmation, when someone we love has just suffered a keen disappointment; the touch of care; the touch with which we greet the bereaved. All these are forms of what we call 'the healing touch'. 'Moved with pity, Jesus stretched out his hand and touched him, and said . . . "Be made clean!" Immediately the leprosy left him, and he was made clean' (Mark 1.41–2). In the literature around AIDS, how important is this reaching out and touching in what counts today as leprosy in the West! But on a much more routine level, a woman friend of mine went to live in India, where the greeting always takes the form of folded hands, the *namaskaram*. It is a beautiful greeting, but it involves no touch. After eighteen months she was feeling absolutely alienated, as if she was from another planet, until the great Mar Thoma theologian M. M. Thomas greeted her one day with a huge bear hug, and restored her world to her.

The point of all this, theologically, is that Christ meets us in our neighbour. We are Christ's hands and feet, Luther used to say. That's usually used in a rather solemn context about mission and diaconate, but think of it literally. Here is this reflection from Anne Briggs to illustrate the point:

> There are moments in church, and moments here and there when I glimpse God – but it's in the arms of my lover, in the heartstopping vulnerability of that moment, when I am loved and accepted for what I am, not what I pretend to be, that I know there is a God who *enjoys* life! In sexual expression I was able to make a dying man feel healed . . . There are terrible sins of omission in the use of our sexuality. There's the refusal to be really vulnerable – there's sexual disdain, and withdrawal (emotional, spiritual as well as physical). For every person whose sexual engagement is without consideration for the other, or for all the others in their life, there's one whose decision not to engage with another is as much about self protection as about virtue.[45]

Taste

In terms of neural equipment, taste is at the bottom of the ladder. Humans have about 10,000 taste buds which die and renew themselves about every ten days. Even today we don't know a huge amount about how taste works, but it appears that different parts of the mouth are more sensitive to different tastes. In a categorization which is echoed today in many Asian cultures, Aristotle distinguished eight basic tastes: sweet and bitter, succulent and salty, astringent, pungent, harsh and acid.[46] Most modern writers distinguish four: sweet, sour, salt, bitter. But as Isabel Allende says, How do they know? How do they classify the metallic taste of fear, the gritty bite of envy, the sparkling flavour of our first kiss?[47] I suspect there are as many tastes as there are varieties of food. In our garden we have twelve apple trees, some of them ancient and unclassified. Each of them has a quite different taste to the other. Blindfold I can tell you which apple comes from which tree, but how can I describe that? There are at least six thousand varieties of apple in the British Isles alone. Martial beautifully describes the kiss of his beloved as tasting of apples. Which apple?

The mutual imbrication of the senses is important here. We can distinguish taste, the sensations which result from contact with the taste buds, and flavour, which includes smell, touch, pressure, pain and sight. The pleasure of taste is not located just in the tongue and the palate, but also in the memory. Jean Dominique Bauby, Editor in Chief of *Elle* magazine, had a massive stroke which resulted in locked-in syndrome, after which he could only communicate by blinking his left eyelid, and he dictated a book in this way. He was fed by a tube into his stomach, but he fantasized food. 'For pleasure I have to turn to the vivid memory of tastes and smells, an inexhaustible reservoir of sensations. Once I was a master at recycling left-overs. Now I cultivate the art of simmering memories . . . Depending on my mood I treat myself to a dozen snails, a plate of Alsatian sausage with sauerkraut, and a bottle of late-vintage golden Gewürztraminer, or else I savour a simple soft-boiled egg with fingers of toast and lightly salted butter. What a banquet!'[48]

As we know from our metaphorical use of the word, taste is basically about discrimination. As Ong points out, the eighteenth-century concern with taste 'derived in great part from the growing number of acts of discrimination which men were having to make . . . With democracy the concern with taste wanes, as "public opinion" is formed to take over regulatory functions.'[49] Taste becomes more important as a metaphor than as a description of intussusception, and we have the distinction of 'people of good taste' as opposed to the vulgar multitude. But already in Scripture taste functions metaphorically: we are urged to 'Taste and see the Lord is good' (Ps. 34.8; Job 20.18), and Jesus is said to have tasted death for all (Heb. 2.9).

The metaphorical sense of taste is inescapable, but I do not want to lose sight of the literal sense. In the days immediately after the Second World War, Karl Barth and a Catholic friend went for a slap-up meal in Paris, which Barth later described as 'a devastating refutation of materialism!' Taste, in its infinite richness, is a sign of grace, the overwhelming abundance and goodness and beauty of what God has given us, which is why it is so beautiful and proper to 'say grace' before meals.

Smell

Like taste, smell cannot be measured scientifically. Aristotle wrote that 'Our power of smell is less discriminating and in general inferior to that of many species of animals; men have a poor sense of smell and our apprehension of its objects is bound up with pleasure and pain, which shows us that in us the organ is inaccurate.'[50] Today, however, we are told that a healthy person may be able to detect between 10,000 and 40,000 different odours. As with taste, there is not a highly developed vocabulary of smell. We say smells are 'like' x and y. But what this means is that it represents the world to us. Far from denigrating smell, it shows it is ineffable. 'How do you describe the aroma of coffee?' asked Wittgenstein. Or of grass after rain, or of pine forests, or of autumn, or of roses? Perhaps we don't have a vocabulary because the phenomenon is so complex. Famously smell is bound up with memory. 'When all else is gone,' said Proust, 'smell and taste bear unflinchingly in the tiny and almost impalpable drop of their essence, the vast structure of recollection.'[51] Helen Keller described smell as 'a potent wizard that transports us across thousands of miles and all the years we have lived'.[52]

In a famous footnote to *Civilization and its Discontents* Freud surmised that civilization began when homo sapiens adopted an upright posture, and sight was privileged over smell.[53] Darwin had already made a similar suggestion in *The Descent of Man*. Both write as archetypal Victorian bourgeois. With his profound classical education I am surprised that Freud did not know the elder Pliny's remark that 'the pleasure of perfume is among the most elegant and also the most honourable enjoyments in life.'[54] Paul seems to have shared the same view because he describes the church as 'the aroma of Christ to God among those who are being saved' (2 Cor. 2.15). Our spending habits show that we agree with Pliny for, as we know, smells are big business, with perfumes, air fresheners, deodorants and polishes. Smell is also used as a moral indicator. Criminal acts, we say, 'stink to high heaven'. 'In this sense,' says Antony Synnot, 'expenditure on colognes, perfumes, after shave and other fragrances is not only an investment in the presentation of the self, but it is also a major component in the moral construction of the self.'[55] By contrast, Francis of Assisi, like many of the early church Fathers, regarded dirt as an insignia of holiness, whilst the seventeenth-century puritans were suspicious of perfume on the ground that it encouraged vanity and licentiousness.[56] And again, in Aldous Huxley's *Brave New World*, on the same moral calculus, fragrance stands for artificial and superficial pleasure, while foulness stands for unpleasant but meaningful reality.[57]

As with taste, the theological significance of smell is, I think, purely and simply as a sign of the economy of grace. Why should we have it? Why should we have roses, and lavender and lilac and honeysuckle? In evolutionary terms these variegated scents seem to play a very small part. There is absolutely no need for them, but, like Lear, God reasons not the need.

Let me now try and bring together these reflections on the senses. In both the Christian and the Greek traditions there has been a suspicion of pleasure, but not consistently. The great seventeenth-century Anglican bishop Jeremy Taylor writes:

> It is lawful when a man needs meat to choose the pleasanter, even merely for their pleasures; that is, because they are pleasant, besides that they are useful; this is as lawful as the smell of a rose, or to lie in feathers, or change the posture of our body in bed for ease, or to hear music, or to walk in gardens rather than in highways; and God has given us leave to be delighted in those things, which he has made to that purpose, that we may also be delighted in him that gives them . . . provided that the pleasure be in its degree moderate, and we temperate in our desires.[58]

God has given us leave to be delighted, that we may be delighted in God who gives them. This has been the substance of much of my argument. But I have also tried to take it further. In speaking of God we cannot do without analogies. We are the aroma of Christ to God, says Paul. We are the temple of God. We are – in a metaphor which has stretched the imaginations of Christians from the moment it was written to the present – the body of Christ. Bodies have senses. No senses, no body; in fact, nobody. Let me try this out, then:

Instruments of grace

The senses are God's palette, and we the brushes.
The senses are God's instruments, and we the players in the orchestra.
The senses are God's spices, and we the banquet.
The senses are God's scents, and we the garden.

In much of what I have said I have in one way or another restated the ancient argument from design, the claim of the psalmist that the heavens are telling the glory of God. But I also want to say that human beings, whom even Barth did not shrink from speaking of as co-creators with God, are as it were God's way of exploring the possibilities and reaches of God's creation, precisely in and through the senses. You will note that in those metaphors or analogies I left out touch. This is because, when we say body we already say touch. Touch, says Walter Ong, is 'the sense which involves me most intimately and also involves what is not me most inescapably'.[59] If you feed the hungry, says Jesus, visit those in prison, help the oppressed, you do it to me. We are the bodies given to convey God's healing touch to the world. Paul's image exercises us so much because it goes beyond metaphor to reality. 'Psychoanalysis has pointed out', says Ong, 'that for the rise of civilization, taboos must be imposed on the senses providing greater bodily pleasures (touch most of all, as well as taste and smell) and more attention must be given to the more sublime (abstract, distancing) senses such as hearing, and, especially, sight.'[60] But civilization is not God's project, *tout court*. The kingdom is God's project, and in that project all the senses are passionately, and sometimes wildly, affirmed. In and through bodies, and through the exercise of our senses, God moves towards the creation of a new world, a world of the celebration and affirmation of bodies, and therefore of the creator who imagined them and gave us them materially, as the consummate sign of the grace of God's essential nature.

2

The senses stilled

More than fifty years after their first appearance, the paintings of Francis Bacon have not lost their power to shock. Take the portraits of Isabel Rawsthorne (Plate 3), for example. Although Rawsthorne said of them that they were 'fabulously accurate', most viewers resile from the bruised flesh and distorted, twisted features.[1] Bacon was a notorious *bon viveur*, not to say *roué*, who all his life denied or at least played down the moral and religious significance of his art. His speech, which is to say his art, however, bewrayeth him. 'In the painting of Francis Bacon,' wrote Alan Ecclestone, 'there is a prolonged courageous attempt to get us to look at life with a new and more serious moral vision.' Bacon refuses to dissemble. 'A search for the truth of man's being takes over; the strains, the misgivings, the fears, the interior twists, are all to be faced and revealed . . . Bacon is so important a painter . . . because his work is expressive of just such scanning in depth that prayer endeavours to do . . . What Bacon can help us to see is how the struggle with chaos and old night goes on in the flesh and spirits of humankind.'[2]

In turning to the theme of disability I hesitated to use Bacon, because of the brutality of his vision, but then I realized that Bacon does not paint disability: he paints so-called 'normal' people and sees the disability in all of them. And more than any other artist he shows us the truth of disabled theologian Nancy Eiesland's remark that 'Embodiment is not a purely agreeable reality; it incorporates profound ambiguity –

sometimes downright distress. There is simply no denying it.'[3] One of Bacon's most acute commentators, Robert Melville, called Bacon 'the greatest painter of flesh since Renoir', but then went on: 'He is the painter of flesh considered as a communal substance . . . the legitimate prey of pain and disease, of ecstasies and torments; obscenely immortal in renewal.'[4]

Rembrandt offers us the alternative vision. Simon Schama, in his wonderful study of the painter, speaks of talk of the compassion of Rembrandt's paintings as a cliché. But clichés are sometimes true. Barth said that Mozart heard 'the peace that passes understanding' and let us hear it in his music; Rembrandt, though, like Mozart, no saint, saw the love of God for the creature, the tender love of the parent in Hosea, of the father of the prodigal, of the God who 'bore Israel' like a mother, and shows us it in his canvases. Where Bacon paints distress, Rembrandt looks at the old, deaf, partially sighted and unglamorous with what can only be called profound compassion. In the last self-portrait (Plate 4), wrote John Berger, 'All has gone except a sense of the question of existence, of existence as a question.'[5] This is not the pity of charitable largesse. This is the compassion born of solidarity, because Rembrandt knew failure, both moral and physical weakness, the death of those he loved most – wives and children – first hand. He looks, if I dare say so, with the eye of incarnation.

Both these painters paint life as it is, warts and all, and without illusions. Now I turn to a promise:

> Then the eyes of the blind shall be opened, and the ears of the deaf unstopped; then the lame shall leap like a deer, and the tongue of the speechless sing for joy . . .
> the ransomed of the Lord shall return and come to Zion with singing;
> everlasting joy shall be upon their heads;

they shall obtain joy and gladness, and sorrow and sighing shall flee away. (Isa. 35.5, 10)

This is the most famous of the messianic promises from Isaiah, through which the Gospels understand Jesus and his work. But how do the deaf, blind and lame in today's world understand these promises? How should they and we? Barbara Patterson believes that it was the experience of martyrdom in the early church which led to the hope that in the next life all bodies with problems would be healed and cured. The long-term consequences for Christianity were, she says, that 'imperfect or troublesome bodies in this world were viewed as partial, marginal, and inadequate. Come the resurrection they would be "fixed".'[6]

For much of the twentieth century, perhaps from the time of Helen Keller onwards, normalization was what guided the approach to handicap. This testament of Colin Barnes, who was born blind, would be typical:

Although both my parents had impairments they did not consider themselves to be disabled people. They did not mix with other disabled people socially and they associated 'disability' with passivity and dependence – qualities which both of them abhorred vehemently . . . my brother was never allowed to help me find things I had lost, and my tendency for blindness-related behaviour was discouraged. The reasoning was . . . so that I would learn to put things where I could find them, and not have to rely on other people to do things for me . . . I only acquired a sense of difference when I went to school.[7]

Today many disabled writers criticize normalization as oppressive. The pressure to be normal, says Sally French, is often at the expense of the disabled person's needs and rights.

With other disabled writers she rejects the view that it is progressive and liberating to ignore difference. Disabled people have a right to be equal and different.[8] Jenny Morris agrees. One of the most oppressive features of the prejudice which disabled people experience, she writes, 'is the assumption that we want to be other than we are, that we want to be normal . . . Do we only have value, even to ourselves, in direct relation to how closely we can imitate "normal" appearance, function, belief and behaviour?'[9]

> We are not normal in the stunted terms the world chooses to define. But we are not obliged to adopt those definitions as standards to which we must aspire, or indeed, regard as something worth having in the first place. Physical disability and illness are an important part of human experience. The non disabled world may wish to try and ignore this and to react to physical difference by treating us as if we are not quite human, but we must recognize that our difference is both an essential part of human experience and, given the chance, can create important and different ways of looking at things.[10]

Frances Young is Professor of Theology at Birmingham University, England, but also the mother of a severely brain-damaged child, Arthur. Insisting that there is no difference between the handicapped and the rest of us, she says, 'dogmatic pursuit of policies of normalisation, is . . . unsatisfactory and may be . . . hurtful . . . We sometimes put the handicapped into a situation of grave risk by pretending that they are no different.'[11]

So I want to ask: Where does this leave the messianic promises? For it seems clear to me that Patterson is wrong, and that the desire for healing of handicap – which you could describe as normalization – long predates early Christian experience of martyrdom, and emerges out of Israel's passion for life. The Hebrew writers, not just Isaiah, but the psalmists and the author of Job, passionately resist anything at all which threatens fullness of life. When Jesus says, in John: 'I have come that they may have life, and have it in all its fullness,' he is speaking out of that tradition (John 10.10). Those things which threaten fullness of life include poverty, hunger, the threat of enemies, illness – but also what today we call impairment or handicap. And we cannot forget that, according to the Gospels, the messianic promises were fulfilled in Jesus – he healed the blind, deaf and lame. Where, then, does this leave handicap as we experience it today?

To begin with I must say a word about terminology and about my sources. As Nancy Eiesland has put it, 'Any theology that seeks access for people with disabilities must necessarily come from . . . within the community of people with disabilities.'[12] In other words, it is essential to allow the disabled to tell the story in their own words even if, as with all other human communities, we will not expect to find complete agreement in the community. It is not for those who are not disabled to colonize this discourse. I shall, therefore, as far as possible allow them to do the talking in what follows.

What language do we use to talk about disability? Nancy Mairs developed MS at the age of 28, and has become progressively wheelchair-bound since. In talking of herself she avoids euphemisms like 'physically challenged'. 'I call myself a cripple . . . because the word is the most accurate and precise I've found, meaning I no longer have full use of my limbs.' The problem with other words, she says, is that they are obstacles to us confronting the radical transformations of our bodies.[13] In a sense they represent that kind of shying away from pain which we instinctively feel before the paintings of Francis Bacon. And for a handicapped person to use the word 'cripple' is perhaps analogous to those members of the homosexual community who have appropriated the formerly derogatory word 'queer' for themselves.

Most mainstream discussion of disability does not take this route. The United Nations statement on disability, written in the dense officialese you expect from such documents, defines *impairment* as 'any loss or abnormality of psychological, physiological or anatomical structure or function'; *disability* as 'any restriction or lack of ability to perform an activity, as a result of an impairment, in a manner or within the range considered normal for a human being'; and *handicap* as the disadvantage the individual encounters, as a result of the impairment and/or disability, when compared with his/her peers.[14] These definitions have not been universally accepted by the disabled, but in general there seems to be an agreement to distinguish between *impairment* on the one hand, which may be either acquired or congenital, and *disability* on the other, which refers to the social consequences of the impairment. Some writers use handicap in this way as well.[15] Impairment is given, we might say, but disability is socially constructed. The theologian Jürgen Moltmann, writing out of an experience of a lifetime living alongside a severely handicapped brother, makes this distinction using two senses of the word 'disability': 'There are burdens that people lay upon other people, and there are burdens with which people are burdened by nature. There are congenital and lifelong disabilities in persons which can neither be corrected or removed. One has to learn to live with them and to love oneself in the midst of them. But there are also the unjust disabilities created by other people and as a result of the laws of public life.'[16]

In this chapter I shall follow the broad distinction between impairment and disability, but I note Susan Wendell's caution that such definitions of impairment and disability 'seem to imply that there is some universal, biologically or medically describable standard of structure, function and human physical ability. But there does not seem to be one.'[17] Realizing that ageing is disabling helps non-disabled people to see that people with disabilities are not 'Other', and this, I have argued, is what Bacon above all helps us to see. Without wanting to minimize the seriousness of disability there is a continuity between the disabled and the non-disabled. As Nancy Mairs puts it, 'Some disabled people call you TAPs, or Temporarily Abled Persons. The fact is that ours is the only minority you can join involuntarily, without warning, at any time.'[18] And for Frances Young: 'Arthur is a whole person as much as I am. I am a handicapped person as much as he is.'[19]

Now to return to my question: how do we understand impairment and disability in the light of the messianic promises and of Jesus' healings? One response begins with the assumption, which I mentioned at the beginning of the first chapter, that the world is a vale of soul-making. Impairment, this response goes, is part of that, for both the impaired and those who care for them, and it can claim exemplary scriptural warrant. For example, in Exodus 4 we read:

> Then YHWH said [to Moses], 'Who gives speech to mortals? Who makes them mute or deaf, seeing or blind? Is it not I, the Lord?' (Ex. 4.11)

And more generally there is the famous verse in Isaiah 45:

> 'I form the light and create darkness,
> I make weal and create woe;
> I YHWH do all these things.' (Isa. 45.7)

Drawing on such texts Simon Horne quotes his disabled partner, Mel, who says, 'My impairment is genetic, so when I was made, God included my impairment, and I have no problems with that. What I do have problems with is the fact that society disables me. God did not make me to be someone who is disabled by society.'[20] And she quotes texts such as Leviticus 19.14:

> 'You shall not revile the deaf or put a stumbling block before the blind; you shall fear your God.'

In these texts we already find anticipated the distinction between impairment and disability which I outlined a moment ago, denouncing the disabling role of society but accepting that impairment comes straight from God. This second assumption is something I find myself unable to share.

When I began my ministry I was chaplain to a small hospital which had two wards for military personnel, some of whom had been there since the First World War. Amongst these was Steve. Steve was 18 when he was parachuted into Arnhem in 1944. A German shell blew away part of his head. Somehow he was got out, brought back to England and put into this hospital, where he lay in a coma for two years. At the end of two years he came round. He was completely paralysed: only his lungs worked. When you visited him you held a cigarette to his lips to enable him to have a smoke. He would tell you of the amazing Ezekiel-like visions he had had during his coma. And he always said: 'Tim, that shell had my name on it. It was intended for me.' I have encountered many similar sentiments since. Making sense of the apparent chaos of reality is one of our deepest needs. We can't bear to believe that everything is purely arbitrary. To believe that God is somehow behind every event can be a comfort, not least to those who are suffering. Nancy Mairs says of her own MS and her husband's melanoma: 'Nothing stands "outside". Everything belongs. We're all weaving some cosmic tapestry of which I've been able to glimpse only a few threads.'[21]

Despite the scriptural warrant for this kind of view, I have to say I can't believe it. It seems to me that in creating the conditions for freedom God has created a world in which randomness and chance play a fundamental part. This does not mean we are abandoned to anarchy and chaos because there is meaning in the larger picture. We can take two analogies to try and understand that. There is the analogy of statistical science, which finds regularity and pattern in what seem to be collections of entirely unrelated facts. That genes may produce uncomfortable results for us, to say the least, is not due to God landing me with a congenital deficiency, but due simply to the way a free creation operates. No malice aforethought, no testing of the human creature, as envisaged in Job chapter 2, is involved.

Another analogy might be Turner's famous practice on varnishing day in the exhibitions of the Royal Academy. Turner liked to explore the analogy of art to creation. He would hang a canvas which seemed to be 'a mere dab of several colours', 'without form and void', like chaos before the creation inviting scorn, scandal and derision. The day before the exhibition was due to open he would come and work intensively at the picture, and miraculously it would suddenly all make sense.[22] I like to think that what we call eschatology, God's drawing of all things together, might be analogous to this practice of Turner's. The final picture will be fabulous, though at the moment we simply can't see that. At the moment all we see are splodges of colour, both light and dark. One thing which is certain about all created reality is that it is finite. Before the end, the Christian faith affirms, things will be 'pulled together' by the divine artist so that they make sense.

If we do not accept the idea that God intended impairment, where does this leave us? First, of course, it leaves us with a stringent critique of a disabling society. There are many aspects to this, and I want to return to the issue of normality, and attitudes towards those who have impairments. Mat Fraser, a disabled actor and comic in Britain, who has recently been given a mainstream show on British television which he has called *Freak Out* records his wish that 'one day the disabled will be just *there*; their disability as invisible as they themselves were previously'. He says of his role in a TV drama in which he plays a drug dealer and his disability is never mentioned: 'Now that's radical.'[23]

Sally French criticizes the philanthropic model of disability adopted by charities which tends to portray disabled people as helpless, sad, courageous and in need of care and protection. Amongst stereotypes of disability she finds their portrayal as pitiable and pathetic 'both patronizing and offensive'. Jenny Morris attacks the tendency of non-disabled people to praise the courage, heroism and achievement of the disabled: 'When people tell you how wonderful you are the judgement that being disabled must be awful and intolerable lies behind it. How can we take pride in ourselves when disability provokes such negative feelings among non disabled people?'[24] In particular she mounts a withering attack on sentimental portrayals of the impaired in the Tiny Tim mould. French argues that disabled charities which emphasize the 'tragedy' of disability 'perpetuate the inaccurate assumption that living with impairment is a life shattering experience. This effectively robs some disabled individuals of the self confidence to overcome disability.'[25] The view that disabled people are helpless and must be cared for fails to acknowledge that with appropriate support people with impairments are able to achieve the same level of autonomy and independence as non-disabled people.[26]

Some of the worst stereotypes of disability come from the religions, and indeed from Scripture. Suffering, including disability, is regularly linked to sin, not least in the story of the man born blind in John 9, though it is vehemently protested in Job. Leviticus debars those with impairments from priestly duties (Lev. 21.18–21). And the psalms make much of virtuous suffering, whilst we are regularly exhorted to care for the lame and the blind, those who cannot help themselves. 'These three themes,' says Eiesland, 'sin and disability conflation, virtuous suffering, and segregationist charity illustrate the theological obstacles encountered by people with disabilities who seek inclusion and justice within the Christian community.'[27] In the same way, in the history of the church, sickness, including physical disability, has served to 'enhance the merits of the just through their patience, to safeguard virtue from pride, to correct the sinner, to proclaim God's glory through miraculous cures, and finally, as the beginning of eternal punishment as in the case of Herod.'[28] To be fair, the solidarity which is really needed has also been there, though only spasmodically. But today, in Jürgen Moltmann's words, we are clearer that 'We cannot get rid of disabilities but we can overcome the disabling of those with disabilities. We can heal the dis-eased relationship between those with and without disabilities. This will occur not through solicitous care and helping but rather through solidarity and living together.'[29]

Stereotypical views of the disabled can lead to shockingly inhuman treatment, and all writers on disability are able to tell stories of disabled groups, or families with a disabled member, being turned away from restaurants or pubs because they will 'upset people'. Such actions cannot be condoned, but at the same time it is important we understand them properly. In the light of one such story Frances Young comments: 'You cannot force integration. Nor can you simply condemn those people who cannot cope with their own feelings . . . The horrific ways in which the handicapped are sometimes treated is the tip of an iceberg of human embarrassment.'[30] To go back to

Francis Bacon, perhaps our reaction to disability is similar to our reaction to his painting, an inability to face the truth about ourselves, about human weakness and the fact that we are all bound up in the bundle of life together.

The disabled themselves, despite rejecting an oppressive 'normality', do not want to be singled out as heroes or as especially 'spiritual' by virtue of their impairment. Nancy Mairs rejected a reviewer who spoke of her 'valiant battle against multiple sclerosis' as 'maudlin'. 'Keep this in mind: I am only doing what I have to do. It's enough.'[31] She will not allow that either she or her husband are heroic. 'Suffering has few heroes, least of all those who wish to live ordinary lives.'[32]

> If a cure were found, would I take it? In a minute. I may be a cripple, but I'm only occasionally a loony and never a saint. Anyway, in my brand of theology God doesn't give bonus points for a limp. I'd take a cure; I just don't need one. A friend who also has MS startled me once by asking, 'Do you ever say to yourself, "Why me Lord?"' 'No Michael, I don't', I told him, 'because whenever I try, the only response I can think of is, "Why not?" If I could make a cosmic deal, who would I put in my place? What in my life would I give up in exchange for sound limbs and a thrilling rush of energy? No one. Nothing. I might as well do the job myself. Now that I'm getting the hang of it.'[33]

To discount attributions of heroism is one thing, but the point of the distinction between impairment and disability is that it is society which is often deeply disabling. To illustrate that we only have to look at the world of the deaf. Sally Sainsbury records the results of studies she did with the deaf in Britain in the 1980s which redefine what we mean by 'exclusion'.[34] Here are some of their voices:

A Deaf[35] retired worker: 'Life is different if you're not

hearing because it's hard to find friends, know what's going on . . . The hearing are different from the deaf and dumb. Most people can't understand what I'm saying . . . Usually I manage to read and write letters, but if they are complicated I go to my sister. Everything takes longer if you are Deaf.'[36]

Mrs Jackson explained, 'Because I can't understand, the greatest problem is being dictated to by others as if I were a child or a young person . . .'

Miss Cox said, 'Because I find lip reading difficult everyone treats me as if I'm mental.'

Mr Douglas summed up the common experience of those in hospitals: 'Because you can't communicate, you miss out on friends and experiences. You don't understand what's going on or what will happen next. There's not much reading and little talk, and everyone pushes you around. [37]

Miss Ayers, aged 35, who lived in the half-way psychiatric hostel, said: 'My mother signs a little bit, but my father doesn't know any signs, and nor do my brother and sister. I find I can talk a little bit to my mother.'

Mrs Salisbury, a widow of 88, who was a patient in a hospital for the mentally ill: 'I had two brothers and a sister. But I didn't really get to know them or my parents.'[38]

The habit of treating the deaf as mentally ill persisted in Britain at least into the 1980s:

One deaf woman with cataracts communicated only by touch; she had no speech, and being illiterate, the only contact she could make with staff was by self mutilation, facial expression and touch. According to the ward sister, she had had no communication of any sort with other patients for several years.[39]

A deaf woman who had been born without eyes was assumed to be subnormal and her parents had been persuaded to send her to a mental handicap hospital. Here, there was no record of a psychological assessment, or attempts to train her to care for herself or to communicate. Now in her mid forties, she was inaccessible and solitary, immobile most of the time in a bent, seated position. She was totally dependent on staff for feeding, dressing, bathing and going to the lavatory.[40]

The study underlines the significance of Ong's point that hearing is the most interior of the senses, and therefore the most profoundly disabling to be without. By the age of three, normal children have 1,000 to 2,000 words. In comparison, the deaf child has fewer than twenty-nine at the age of four.[41] Two-fifths of the deaf people Sainsbury interviewed found daily chat difficult, and a fifth found it impossible. As many as two-thirds of deaf people never attempted to discuss subjects such as politics, religion or sport with hearing people. Almost a third of the deaf were barely if at all literate, at most able to make some attempt at writing, but always referring correspondence to hearing people for advice and at worst unable to devise letters of any description except by copying word for word.[42]

The conclusion of Sainsbury's study was that 'The deaf lived lives which had much of the appearance of those of the hearing, but in practice, they were not part of the hearing community: the deaf lived lives which were parallel to those of the hearing. And in terms of social activities they were enabled to do so by the existence of the deaf community, which, in large measure, was sustained and reinforced by the existence of deaf clubs.'[43]

That the frankly appalling experience of exclusion revealed by Sainsbury's study is not inevitable is made clear by the experience of Martha's Vineyard, in New England. From the seventeenth century to the early years of the twentieth, the population of Martha's Vineyard manifested an extremely high rate of profound hereditary deafness.

> In stark contrast with the experience of most deaf people in our own society, the Vineyarders who were born deaf were so thoroughly integrated into the daily life of the community that they were not seen, and did not see themselves, as handicapped or a group apart. Deaf people were included in all aspects of life, such as town politics, jobs, church affairs and social life . . . On the Vineyard, hearing and deaf Islanders alike grew up speaking sign language. This unique socio-linguistic adaptation meant that the usual barriers to communication between the hearing and the deaf, which so isolate many deaf people today, did not exist.[44]

This existence of parallel worlds brings us back to the question of normality.

Collectively, says one study of deafness, the deaf 'are torn between affirming and bemoaning their deafness, between looking to fellow members for self identity and self esteem and looking to the larger world which is all around them.'[45] One manifestation of this ambivalence is the phenomenon Goffman, in his study of stigma, called 'passing', i.e. passing as normal. Because of the great rewards in being considered normal, he says, almost all persons who are in a position to will 'pass' on some occasions. The example he gives is of a deaf person who, when invited out to dinner, would either sit next to someone with a strong voice, choke or cough if asked a direct question, ask someone to tell a story she had already heard or ask questions to which she already knew the answer.[46] Today, as I noted earlier, there seems to be a consensus that it is necessary to insist on equality and difference. In Britain, for example, there is now a demand that British Sign Language be treated on a par with any other language.

If profound deafness raises sharp questions about exclusion and provides us with a paradigm of how society may be disabling, other questions are posed by mental handicap. Frances Young's son, Arthur, was severely brain damaged as a result of a placenta which was too small and inefficient, which deprived him of necessary oxygen during his development in the womb.[47] In her account of her attempts to come to terms with this and to celebrate Arthur, alongside her other children, Young faces the hard questions such handicap raises. According to the 'vale of soul-making' theodicy God intended people to grow to maturity in faith and love. But what about those who are incapable of doing so? We are a psychosomatic whole and a damaged brain means that the whole personality is damaged and lacks potential for development.[48] What about autism, a condition in which the person finds it impossible to relate to the external world or to other people?[49] There are people, Young reminds us, 'like Arthur and more limited than Arthur, of whom it is very difficult to speak of some kind of "person" distinct from the brain damaged body . . . There is no "ideal Arthur" somehow trapped in this damaged physical casing.'[50] I shall return later to the implications of these questions for our understanding of the resurrection.

These questions, and the exclusion of the deaf, put in sharp focus Jurgen Moltmann's suggestion that disability should be understood as a gift of the Holy Spirit. 'Every disability is also a gift of the Holy Spirit. It is a gift that we do not discover only because we are so focussed on what a person is missing . . . Having a disability, whatever form it might take, is also a gift of the Holy Spirit, if through and in the disability one is called to be God's image and glory on earth.'[51]

How far are we able to pursue this suggestion? Does it have

any limits? I recall a former student of mine in India, severely disabled, who in a discussion of resurrection said: 'If resurrection means I keep this body, I don't want resurrection.' What about Sally Sainsbury's forty-year-old woman, deaf, and born without eyes? Can we really speak of that as a gift? What about those unable to grow? And how are we to distinguish between mental handicap, on the one hand, and a mental illness like paranoid schizophrenia on the other? Supposing that such a condition is genetically caused, is it not both an illness and a handicap, and a profoundly disabling one at that, because it constitutes a danger to society? We could not regard such a condition as a gift, but then where do we draw the line? Is the capacity to act morally the crucial indicator? If so, where would it leave severely brain damaged people like Frances Young's son? When Diane Devries was born without legs and with only stumps for arms, her doctor fainted.[52] She is amusing about that, but in all my experience of childbirth one of the first questions those not in the labour room ask is: 'Are mother and baby all right?' If the answer is affirmative, very commonly people say 'Thank God'. But then, Susan Wendell asks, is saying 'Everyone wants a healthy baby' morally and politically similar to saying, 'Everyone wants a white baby?' 'If not, how is it different? Is there as much reason to preserve the functional impairments and structural imperfections of human bodies as there is to preserve their genetic diversity?'[53] How would you answer that in the light of the need first to affirm the disabled, and at the same time to make sense of the messianic promises?

The disabled themselves refuse any romanticization of disability. R. A. Scott notes that it is supposed that the blind dwell in a world that is apart from and beyond the one ordinary people inhabit. 'This world, which is believed to be less gross and materialistic than our own, is said to be infused with a spirituality that gives its inhabitants a peculiar purity and innocence of mind. Those who live in the world of the blind are believed capable of experiencing unique inner feelings and rising to aesthetic heights that are beyond the abilities of all but the most unusual of sighted men.'[54] But it seems that there is no evidence to support the claim that the sensory apparatus of the blind child is actually more acute; she just uses the senses she has more effectively. Sighted children, when blind-folded, often do better at tactile tasks because sight helps us integrate information from all our senses.[55]

Setting aside any false romanticism, it is true that some disabled people are able to understand their impairment in a positive sense. Nancy Mairs found herself compelled to examine 'what about life-with-MS . . . is worth having. And celebrating.'[56]

> If anyone had told me that at the age of 43 I would be crippled and George have cancer, and my family dying I would have cried out 'Oh no, I could never survive such pain!'. But if anyone had told me, in the presence of these realities, I would find myself, without warning, pierced by joy, I would have been stunned speechless, certain that my informant was either perverse or outright mad.[57]

This note of celebration takes us back to the idea of the senses as God's means of celebrating and exploring God's world. What about impairment can we regard as a means of celebration in the same way?

In answering this question I bear in mind David Pailin's crucially important warning that we must not seek to understand handicap in terms of what it makes possible for others, which rests on what he calls the 'contributory theory of human worth'.[58] According to this theory what grounds our worth is what we contribute to human society. Handicapped people contribute, the argument goes, by allowing others to care for them. Not so, says Pailin, for ultimately this depersonalizes us all, and degrades both carer and cared for. Rather, worth is bestowed by being loved, wanted and respected. Worth 'is given to each person by the way that others, including – and ultimately – God, regard him or her'.[59]

Presupposing this, it remains true that handicap, like every other aspect of human life, has its own place in the overall human economy, those aspects of being human which call us to celebrate. To affirm that is not to go back on the view that God does not design or cause handicap as a way of 'testing our mettle', or for any other purpose. That would be to write the 'contributory theory' into the very structure of the universe. Rather, given the world as it is, we learn to give thanks for what our neighbours, including our handicapped neighbours, give us. In the first place, then, I would say this was the chance to learn about the *dependency* and *interdependency* proper to human life. In the Christian tradition a positive value is set on weakness (1 Cor. 1.26), and Paul lists setbacks and sadnesses amongst gifts of Spirit (2 Cor. 4.7). It was precisely this which was anathema to Nietzsche, but, as Frances Young says, 'Handicapped people remind us that life is not all go-getting and individual achievement. There are more fundamental human values. Handicap demands mutual support, a sense of communal sharing. It challenges our selfishness and our ambition and sectional loyalties.'[60] And Susan Wendell notes that 'An adult who needs someone else's help to eat, wash, dress and use the toilet may see very clearly how a culture despises this kind of dependency, but also how the same culture promotes the self deception that "independent" adults do not need each other's help.'[61] The reality of handicap is, then, 'a critique of our illusions'.[62] Remember, we are TAPS, temporarily abled persons. Whether we like it or not, illness and handicap are a fundamental feature of the world God saw and pronounced 'good'.

Simon Horne suggests that, 'Living dependently is living in the image of God.' He argues this on the grounds that God has chosen to be to an extent dependent on us, dependent on human response to promptings of our consciences. 'In this dependence on us God experiences both impairment and disability.'[63]

We have to recognize, however, a negative side to dependency. Scott comments that the disability of blindness is a learned social role. 'There is nothing inherent in the condition of blindness that requires a person to be docile, dependent, melancholy, or helpless.'[64] On the other hand, 'The blind person is . . . by virtue of his dependency, the subordinate in a power relationship. As a rule, none of the alternatives available to subordinates in power relationships are open to him. He cannot forgo the service required, since performing important activities of daily life depends on the cooperation of sighted persons. It is unlikely that he will turn elsewhere . . . Finally, he cannot very well rely on force to have favours done for him. He is, therefore, locked into a position of compliance.'[65]

So disability can teach us about both true and false dependence. But secondly, it can be in its own way *enabling*. Nancy Mairs asks, 'What's wrong with "difficulty"? . . . I want to redeem it, as both a word and a concept. I want to speak it out loud, without apology, in the same matter of fact tone I'd use to say, "I prefer black cats to spotted ones" . . . And then I want to figure out how I can not merely admit to having a difficult life but also use the difficulties I've acknowledged to enrich the life.'[66]

One may cry harder in the clutches of a troubled existence, but one may laugh harder as well . . . In addition to making me more humorous I think the difficult life has made me more attentive . . . the most valuable response I've developed is gratitude . . . What I'm grateful for is that, in spite of having MS, I've fulfilled ambitions I never dreamed I would.[67]

Sally French documents how many health professionals have found disability enabling. For example, a psychiatrist with MS finds that this has helped her to become more sensitive to the needs of others and speaks of herself as being doubly qualified, 'firstly as a patient and secondly as a doctor – the order is important'.[68] A deaf therapist commented that 'they don't see me as a health professional who knows it all who doesn't really understand, they see me as a disabled person'. A blind social worker reports being able to address clients: ' "I'll help you but there are certain ways in which you are going to have to help me" and the client doesn't feel totally taken over or totally worthless'.[69] All these are examples of the 'wounded healer', the tradition which recognizes that only those who know sickness from the inside can heal, and exemplified, of course, by Christ.

Further than that, there are profound ways in which handicap can enrich our lives. Frances Young says of her relation with Arthur: 'Where I minister to others, Arthur ministers to me. He shows me what life is about, brings me down to basics, gives me peace, helps me to resolve the tensions, and it is with him that I find the fruits of the Spirit.'[70] We have to realize, she says, that handicap is different, not 'sub'. 'The basic trustfulness, lack of inhibitions, and that indefinable virtue – simplicity – often seen in the mentally handicapped may be the very qualities that it would be criminal to educate out of them.'[71] On these lines the mother of a Downs syndrome child said, on her child's twenty-second birthday:

What I've enjoyed about Kathleen is how she appreciates everything, life in general. No matter what she got she always appreciated everything. She thought as much of getting a card as she did of getting a box of chocolates. There's always been this great love and affection between us.[72]

Thirdly, handicap constitutes a critique of idolatry of the young, fit, healthy body. Wendell writes: 'I regard the current level of cultural idealization, objectification, quest for perfection, and demand for control of the body as a collective sickness of the soul, and an alienation from experience and reality. I believe that people with and without disabilities would benefit from lessening the desire to control one's body and increasing the desire to live in respectful harmony with it.'[73] Moltmann agrees, arguing that the values of health, achievement and beauty can make people inhuman. 'Persons who equate being human with being healthy cannot abide seeing a sick person. Persons who identify being human with power to achieve will despise weak persons. Those who seek out beauty in persons will regard every disability as ugly.[74] Implied in any idealization of the body is the rejection of some kinds of bodies or some aspects of our normally recalcitrant bodily life. In a society where denial of our particular bodies and questing for a particular body is 'normal', respect for handicapped and non-ideal bodies is an act of resistance and liberation.[75] Over against this disabling ideal we have to set an understanding of true health as 'the strength to live, the strength to suffer and the strength to die'.[76]

There is a mutually illuminating relationship between these observations on handicap in community and Christian understandings of both what it means to be human and our understanding of God. As Eiesland puts it, 'Our bodies participate in the *imago Dei* not *in spite of* our impairments and contingencies but *through* them.'[77] We can say this because, if the Christian revelation is true, then God chooses to heal us through weakness and through the cross. 'Christians do not have an able bodied God as their primal image. Rather, the Disabled God promising grace through a broken body is at the centre of piety, prayer, practice and mission.'[78] It was an axiom of fourth-century Christology that 'Not assumed is not healed.' This was an argument for Christ's full assumption of human flesh. The implication of this is, says Moltmann, that 'The eternal God took on not only the limited and mortal aspects of humanity but also the disabled, sick, weak, helpless and lifeless aspects of humanity. He took on our disabilities and made them an expression of his own pain. It is by taking on every sickness and every care and making them his own sufferings and his own cares that God heals all sicknesses and all cares.'[79] So impairment, or handicap, is part of the structure of redemption. This does not call into question the idea that God explores the creation through our senses, but it does put it in a radically different light. It means, for example, that hedonism, as a religion of the celebration of the senses and nothing more, could never be our gospel. It means, as we see in the New Testament, that eros, for all its glory, can never be all that we mean by love. It means that there are depths plumbed by difficulty which are not plumbed by ease.

So let me return to Wendell's question whether there would ever be a reason for genetic screening-out of handicap. I find myself saying 'No'. There is something deeply depressing, and deeply antithetical to the Christian revelation, in the vision of a race of nothing but super athletes with high IQs. For one thing, I wouldn't have any part in it. More seriously, the fourth-century theologians believed that Christ's assumption of humanity had implications for the whole human race. This means that 'in truth there is no such thing as a reduced or disabled life. In its own way, each life is divine life and must be experienced and respected as such.'[80] This is not to say that research to overcome MS or other disabling diseases is mistaken. Of course it is not, but has to be recognized, along with the support and love of the community, as a continuation of the healing Jesus practised in his ministry. What is vital, however, is to continue this research without calling into question the value of life of those who are disabled.

Finally, then, what about the resurrection? We know that, as psychosomatic beings, our bodies are part of who we are, part of our 'fundamental structure of being'. If handicap is part of that then it must have some relation to our existence beyond death. 'Whatever transformations may occur as a person grows in holiness or moves into a different mode of existence,' writes Pailin, 'it is essentially that person as she or he is at the present moment, and not a different one or a potential one, who is embraced by the divine.'[81] To think otherwise is to think that the handicapped person does not have worth to God as they are right now. This insistence seems to me, however, to overlook the role that dream, vision and hope plays in our 'gestalt', that 'me-ness' which will be raised, and which is not simply identical with our physical or moral selves. I think of Nesan, my Sri Lankan student, who was determined more by his spirit than his physical frame.[82] 'What is sown is perishable,' says Paul, 'what is raised is imperishable. It is sown in dishonour, it is raised in glory. It is sown in weakness, it is raised in power. It is sown in a physical body, it is raised a a spiritual body' (1 Cor. 15.42–44). This transfiguration of everything that we are, and of the whole creation, is surely the key to our thinking about resurrection:

Arise, shine; for your light has come,
and the glory of the Lord has risen upon you. (Isa. 60.1)

This radiance, the author of Revelation implies, will bathe the whole created world, and in it we will all be renewed (Rev. 21.23). In that renewal, I am sure, there will be neither impairment nor handicap but, as the Athanasian creed put it, 'one equal glory'.

Plate 1: John Constable, *Marine Parade and Chain Pier at Brighton*,
© Tate, London 2001.

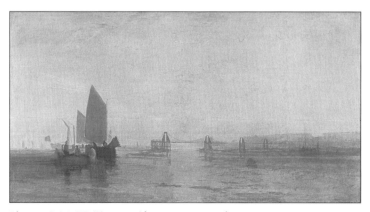

Plate 2: J. M. W. Turner, *Chain Pier at Brighton*,
© Tate, London 2001.

Plate 3: Francis Bacon, *Portrait of Isabel Rawsthorne*, © Estate of Francis Bacon/ARS, NY, and DACS, London 2001.

Plate 4: Rembrandt van Rijn, *Self-Portrait Aged 63*, © National Gallery, London.

Plate 5: Velazquez, *Innocent X*, © Galleria Doria-Pamphili, Rome.

Plate 6: Caravaggio, *John the Baptist*, © The Nelson-Atkins Museum of Art, Kansas City, Missouri (Purchase: Nelson Trust) 52-25 Photography by Robert Newcombe & Edward Robinson.

Plate 7: Georges Grosz, *The Painter of the Hole*, © President and Fellows of Harvard College.

3

Sins of the flesh?

Velazquez (1599–1659) was from his twenties attached to a
Spanish court of extreme decadence, and throughout his life
aspired to be ennobled, an honour he was not granted until a
few months before his death. Before it could happen he had to
prove that his family on both sides was untainted by Moorish
or Jewish blood and that he had never indulged in a menial
craft, for example by selling paintings. 'So far as the scanty
records reveal,' remarks Madlyn Kahr, 'he was perfectly
adapted to the social order in which he lived.'[1] Nothing, you
would think, could more damage artistic integrity. Yet look at
the picture of Innocent X (Plate 5), one of the greatest of his
portraits. The Pope exclaimed, on being shown the picture:
'It's too real!' Without being a tacit satire, it is a study of wary
and ruthless power which would not, and did not, hesitate to
act in its own interest. Did Dostoevsky know this painting
when he wrote the story of the Grand Inquisitor? If not, it
would certainly have fitted the bill: what this man believes in
is the authority conferred by office. If you want a depiction of
spiritual sin, this is it. Not for nothing was Bacon obscssed by
it, producing his own version repeatedly, in which the inner
cruelty is but made explicit.

If you want sins of the flesh, by contrast, you can turn to
Caravaggio (1571–1610), possibly an influence on Velazquez,
whose self-portraits and young males positively ooze
sensuality. Above all there are his depictions of Bacchus, in
which the half-parted lips are an obvious invitation, and in

which overt sexual symbolism abounds. The Uffizi Bacchus did not become famous until the twentieth century, and it seems that in the sixteenth century it was simply too explicit for anyone to display. Even Caravaggio's John the Baptist (Plate 6) is turned into a brooding adolescent, a sort of James Dean character, of tremendous erotic power. Amongst the painters only Courbet approaches Caravaggio for his decadent eroticism.

These two painters seem clearly to show that there are sins of the flesh and sins of the spirit. But are there such things as sins of the flesh? To this question I expect two quite different answers. Some will answer, 'Of course there are.' Paul condemned gluttony, lust, drunkenness and adultery as 'sins of the flesh'. He tells us in Philippians that those who make bodily desires their god are going to end up in hell (Phil. 3.18–20). *Porneia*, sometimes translated 'sexual immorality', and sometimes 'fornication' is roundly condemned, especially by Paul. In the New Testament we find a clear division between flesh and spirit. Jesus says that the spirit is willing but the flesh is weak (Mark 14.38). Paul says that flesh wars against the Spirit (Gal. 5.16–17), mind against body. 'With my mind (*nous*)', he says, 'I am a slave to the law of God, but with my flesh I am a slave to the law of sin . . . those who live according to the flesh set their minds on the things of the flesh, but those who live according to the Spirit set their minds on the things of the Spirit' (Rom. 7.25; 8.5). For this reason we are told we should mortify the senses. The author of 1 Peter speaks of fleshly desires which wage war against the soul (1 Pet. 2.11). In 1 John we are told:

> Do not love the world or the things in the world. The love of the Father is not in those who love the world; for all that is in the world – the desire of the flesh, the desire of the eyes, the pride in riches – comes not from the Father but from the world. (1 John 2.15)

Sins of the flesh?

Hardly surprising that historians should tell us that Christianity has, for most of its history, cultivated hatred of the body.[2] Even the most nuanced treatment of the body in early Christian teaching agrees that 'In all later Christian writing after Paul the notion of "the flesh" suffused the body with disturbing associations: somehow, as "flesh", the body's weaknesses and temptations echoed a state of helplessness, even of rebellion against God, that was larger than the body itself.'[3] The case looks unanswerable.

Others, however, will respond like this: In the major theological passages which speak of 'flesh' the word does not mean our bodies and the things we do with them. For getting on for a century scholars have been telling us that 'flesh' in the New Testament is a code word for humankind organized against God. Thus Rudolf Bultmann writes that flesh represents 'trust in oneself as being able to procure life . . . through one's strength and accomplishment'.[4] And a more recent specialist study of this terminology confirms that *sarx* for Paul is not rooted in sensuality but rather in religious rebellion in the form of self-righteousness.[5] If you look at what Paul, who is responsible for the vast bulk of uses of the word 'flesh', describes as sins of the flesh, then, yes, of course you do find immorality and licentiousness, drunkenness and carousing, but you also find idolatry, sorcery, enmity, strife, jealousy, anger, quarrels, dissensions, factions and envy (Gal. 5.19–21). What connection does most of that list have with our bodies, specifically? When *porneia* is mentioned it often comes in a list of other sins such as evil intentions, murder, theft, false witness and slander (Matt. 15.19). It would be quite wrong to regard the New Testament as an extended sermon about sexual sin, like Augustine's 'On Marriage and Concupiscence'. In fact, slander, malice and the sins of Mammon figure still more extensively.

Moreover, talk of 'sins of the flesh' presupposes a dualism

which Scripture eschews. 'The person thinks with his body,' as Moltmann puts it. 'The brain and the bodily organs instruct one another.'[6] Alternatively one can argue that there cannot be specifically sins of the flesh because everything goes through our head, and Jesus recognized this in highlighting the *intention* behind adultery (Matt. 5.27–8). Yes, he talks about a look, but that's as far as the flesh goes. It's really about the imagination, what the rabbis called the *yetzer ha'ra*, the evil intent. As it says in Genesis, 'the imagination (*yetzer*) of humankind is evil from its youth up' (Gen. 8.21). These alternative approaches illustrate the fact that we are, in Terry Eagleton's words, 'cusped between nature and culture', a fact which Paul explores in Romans 7 and Freud in his case studies.[7] As with any arch, the danger is that we can easily fall apart.

The marginal significance of 'sins of the flesh' is confirmed when we look at the tradition of the seven deadly sins. Only two refer specifically to the body – lust and gluttony. The rest – anger, greed, envy and sloth – are what you might call 'spiritual' sins, and topping the list is pride, which both Christians and rabbis have always agreed is the paramount sin. So the body, actually, is not a particular focus for sin.

The first, and probably mainstream, view of sins of the flesh would be nervous of any theology of the senses, finding in them an occasion for sin. John Chrysostom said that each sense must fast from its own particular evil.[8] Following his advice I shall look at each of the senses, and try to see what that particular evil might be, and on which side of the divide the scale would come down.

Sight

Once, in the 1960s, I was on an all-male pilgrimage which stopped at a tiny cider pub in a remote Norfolk hamlet. On the wall was a girlie calendar, extremely decorous by today's standards, but nevertheless intended to be titillating. As we entered, our Roman Catholic chaplain, who went on to become archbishop of Birmingham, roared: 'Gentlemen: Custody of eyes!'

Throughout the patristic and medieval period custody of eyes was a fundamental precept. Augustine condemned ocular desire which diverts our eyes from more spiritual concerns.[9] Chrysostom warned that unchastened gazing is the greatest snare. Francis would never lift his eyes from the ground in the presence of a woman. Curiously, for all its hostility to Christian moralizing this is one area where contemporary secular thought has endorsed the Christian tradition. In a remark which could have come from any of these church Fathers, Norman Bryson says that 'the life of vision is one of endless wanderlust, and in its carnal form the eye is nothing but desire'.[10] All these writers are men. What do women think?

Much feminist thought attacks the objectifying, reifying power of the male gaze. 'Women's desire', says Luce Irigaray, 'does not speak the same language as man's desire. In this logic the prevalence of the gaze . . . is particularly foreign to women's eroticism. Women find pleasure more in touch than in sight.'[11] She would hardly agree with Bryson's universalizing account of vision. For her it is specifically the male gaze which is the problem, one of patriarchy's instruments of power. 'More than any other sense, the eye objectifies and it masters. It sets at a distance, and maintains a distance. In our culture the predominance of the look over smell, taste, touch and hearing has brought about an impoverishment of bodily relations.'[12]

Irigaray's point about the male gaze as opposed to the role of touch in women's eroticism seems to be confirmed by the fact that the vast bulk of the purchasers and users of visual pornography, which is surely the paradigm of the objectifying gaze, appear to be men. It is claimed that an increasing number of women now use it – in the United States it is said that this is now up to 20% of the market, and there is a specialist women's erotic video firm. Given that reality is socially constructed, we might expect equality feminism to have something like this result. I am focusing on visual pornography because, of course, much pornography is literary, and this long pre-dates the top-shelf magazine and the video. These are only possible in the high-tech consumer society.

In Christian and theological circles pornography is often condemned but rarely discussed. The reason is obvious: the condemnation of *porneia* in the letters of Paul, and Jesus' remark about the adulterous gaze. If you want a command ethic, there it is. Nothing could be clearer. Nevertheless, there are at least two good reasons for discussing it. First, visual pornography is big business in our society. In the United States it grosses more than the music and movie industries combined; in Britain 2.5 million top-shelf magazines are sold monthly, and there is an estimated readership of 5 million, a huge percentage of the adult population.[13] Worldwide in 1999 its takings were estimated at $11 billion. And as Laura Kipnis puts it, 'pornography's not going away anytime soon'.[14] We cannot bury our heads in the sand about this phenomenon, but had better try to understand what is going on. Secondly, in its exploration of fantasy, pornography in many ways gets close to the heart of the human condition, something that both the desert Fathers and Augustine realized.

There is an ongoing debate about this industry, not least within feminism, and, at the risk of over-simplification I will try to distinguish three positions, largely within the feminist discussion.

First, there are those feminists, like Catherine Itzin and Andrea Dworkin, who argue that pornography is the theory of which rape is the practice, and that there is no harmless pornography. All pornography perpetuates sexual inequality and violence against women.[15] 'Pornography is propaganda against women. It is a practice which perpetuates sexism, sex discrimination and sexual violence . . . Sexual equality depends on the elimination of pornography.'[16] Pornography is a key part of the maintenance of male power.[17]

In Christian circles it is likely that this view is taken for granted, but Laura Kipnis's brilliant study of transvestite, fat and geriatric pornography calls it into question.[18] Much pornography is not centrally about women at all; much is only vestigially about sex. Many would argue that the portrayal of violence in mainstream cinema, much of which has no overt sexual reference, is the most worrying form of pornography. Much sexual pornography is about transgressing boundaries in some way or other, and in particular about upsetting middle-class cultural codes. Pornography, Kipnis insists, is essentially about fantasy, and its role is to insist on a sanctioned space for this.

Secondly, there are those who, like Gloria Steinem and Kate Millett, make a distinction between pornography and erotica. 'We got pornography,' said Kate Millett, 'What we needed was eroticism.' However, 'There is some usefulness in explicitness . . . it can help us get over dreadful patriarchal ideas that sex is evil and that the evil in it is women.'[19]

Gloria Steinem argues that pornography is about dominance whilst erotica is about mutuality. In erotica 'the images may be diverse, but there is usually a sensuality and touch and warmth, an acceptance of bodies and nerve endings'.[20] The philosopher Roger Scruton argues that pornography is the perspective of the keyhole whereas the erotic work, 'is one which invites the reader to re-create in imagination the first person point of view of someone party to an erotic encounter'.[21]

This distinction between pornography and erotica is queried from both left and right. On the one hand what is called 'erotica' seems designed to titillate, and therefore fulfils the same function as pornography, whilst on the other hand Linda Williams argues that 'The very notion of erotica as "good", clean, non explicit representations of sexual pleasure in opposition to dirty, explicit pornographic ones is false. The erotic and the pornographic interact in hard core. The one emphasizes desire, the other satisfaction. Depending on who is looking, both can appear dirty, perverse, or too explicit.'[22] Relatedly, Linda Nead argues that art and pornography cannot be isolated, but must be recognized as elements 'within a cultural continuum that distinguishes good and bad representations of the female body, allowable and forbidden forms of cultural consumption, and that which defines what can or cannot be seen'.[23]

Thirdly, there are those feminists like Linda Williams, Lynne Segal, Laura Kipnis and Angela Carter who are not prepared to be dismissive about pornography.

Linda Williams has made a study of so-called hard core pornography, and argues that it is not the enemy. 'Neither are fantasies, which by definition are based on unruly desires rather than politically correct needs. The one speaks to us about bodies and organs; the other describes the often circuitous roles these bodies and organs play in satisfying our desires. Pornography speculates about both.'[24]

For Lynne Segal polymorphous pornography deconstructs male power: 'The more discourses there are around sex, the more sexist oppositions between male and female, active and passive, subject and object, begin to break down. Oddly, this is most clear in pornographic s/m.'[25]

According to Angela Carter, 'A moral pornographer might use pornography as a critique of current relations between the sexes.' Carter argues that his purpose would be the demystification of the flesh and the making clear of the real relations between persons. Such a pornographer, she says, 'would not be an enemy of women, . . . because he might begin to penetrate to the heart of the contempt for women that distorts our culture'. 'Sexual relations between men and women always render explicit the nature of social relations in the society in which they take place and, if described explicitly, will form a critique of those relations.'[26]

As you see, at the heart of all three of these positions is not the flesh, as such, but power, and therefore relationship. This seems to be what much of the moral argument is really about. Can there be depictions of the naked body which do not raise the question of power in a problematic way? John Berger famously argued that in the European tradition there were 'perhaps a hundred' nudes in which the painter's personal vision, his love for his subject, made reification impossible.[27] This has been challenged by feminist art critics like Linda Nead, but to my mind there are some works of art, like Michelangelo's *David,* or Rembrandt's picture of *Bathsheba* in the Louvre, which simply cannot be regarded as pornographic. By that I mean that you cannot view these works concentrating primarily on the genitals; nothing in the pose of either figure is about sexual display; their intrinsic dignity resolutely denies the possibility of their use for masturbatory fantasy. There used also to be, and perhaps still is, a magazine devoted to photographs from nudist camps, called *Health and Education,* whose photographs, far from being erotic, were slightly embarrassing, as if one had stumbled into a shower where someone had forgotten to lock the door. The difference of these photographs from pornography seems to be bound up with intention, the posing of the body as a form of sexual invitation; and perhaps this applies also to John Berger's canon. But are images of the nude which do stimulate desire necessarily wrong? William Countryman, in his important essay on sex and property ethics, *Dirt, Greed and Sex*, argued that erotic literature and art form a widespread and diverse phenomenon which may at times be contrary to Christian ethics, particularly when they set up idolatrous ethical standards which treat the self and its sexual gratification as the final goal of existence, or when they present as acceptable the degradation of adults or abuse of children, but 'The pleasure attached to explicit sexual portrayals in words or pictures should be accepted as the powerful ally of any effort to teach the responsible use of so beautiful a thing.'[28] Is it the old suspicion of pleasure which leads to our condemnation of pornography, and, by contrast, is the widespread use of it not the inevitable correlate of a hedonist society?

As I noted, it is easy for the Christian to make a blanket condemnation of pornography on the grounds of the New Testament condemnation of *porneia*, but Laura Kipnis's demonstration of the class bias of most pornography critique, and Linda Nead's account of the continuum between art and pornography, at the very least problematizes that. Kipnis argues that psychoanalysis is the route through which we have to try and understand pornography and that it is a powerful aid in helping us to understand 'that amalgam of complexes, repressions, and identifications we call "me"'.[29] In this she is at one with the desert Fathers, if Peter Brown is to be believed. For them sexual temptation was not the biggest issue, but nevertheless the pervasiveness and resilience of sexual fantasy 'served as barium traces, by which the Desert Fathers mapped out the deepest and most private recesses of the will'.[30] This raises the question of where the Christian, and especially the Augustinian, account of what it means to be human stands in relation to the light psychoanalysis has thrown on repression and fantasy. Freud and his successors have made clear that none of us exist without fantasy and that it is a fundamental part of the human condition. Fantasy, we should be clear, is not purely, or even predominantly, sexual: as children we fantasize ourselves as sports or ballet heroes, or as rock stars; and how many million people around the world dream what they will do with their winnings in the run-up to every Lottery draw? The desert Fathers, and Augustine, sought to tame fantasy by the will, in Freudian terms, repressing and sublimating it. Augustine famously argued that in paradise sexual intercourse was solely a matter of will, and that concupiscence did not come into it. There is a deep suspicion of fantasy in the Christian tradition resting on its self-indulgence, its unreality and, if it concerns a living person, the non-consensual element of it.[31] Fantasy, you could say, points you away from the real task of the Kingdom of God. But how different is it from play? Indeed, is it not a – solitary – form of play? Criticism of its unreality misses the mark because, as Kipnis points out, what we are dealing with is psychic reality, and efforts to discipline it may result in repressions which do more harm than the original fantasy itself. As she says, perhaps 'when issues of pleasure, plenitude, and freedom are articulated more frequently in places other than fantasy genres like pornography they won't need to find their expression only in these coded and pornographic forms'.[32] Perhaps, but perhaps not, for the issue of transgression, of shock and crossing boundaries, is clearly central not only to pornography but to much sexual behaviour.[33]

Angela Carter argues that a moral pornographer might aim at the total demystification of the flesh. Is that something we should welcome? John Berger speaks of the loss of mystery involved in nudity, and this loss is an aspect of one argument against not just visual but all pornography which I have not mentioned yet, and which, to my knowledge, plays a rather small part in the feminist discussion. Its most articulate voice is George Steiner, and I call it the privacy argument.

In an essay called *Night Words*, Steiner argues that sexual relations are, or should be, one of the citadels of privacy, the nightplace where we must be allowed to gather the splintered, harried elements of our consciousness to some kind of inviolate order and repose.

> It is in sexual experience that a human being alone, and two human beings in that attempt at total communication which is also communion, can discover the unique bent of their identity. That we can find for ourselves, through imperfect striving and repeated failure, the words, the gestures, the mental images which set the blood to racing. In that dark and wonder ever-renewed both the fumblings and the light must be our own. The new pornographers subvert this last, vital privacy; they do our imagining for us. They take away the words that were of the night and shout them over the roof tops, making them hollow. The images of our love making, the stammerings we resort to in intimacy, come pre-packaged.[34]

Kipnis could argue that Steiner is a typical high culture theorist, unwilling and perhaps unable to understand the popular culture to which pornography belongs. She could point out that all our cultural responses are learned, and to that extent come pre-packaged. We do not object, for example, to learning the grammar of romantic love from John Donne or Jane Austen. Why do we single out this other form of intimacy? Sympathetic as I am to Kipnis's class analysis it seems to me that Steiner's plea for privacy is on to something, particularly in the context of the World Wide Web, when people compete to put the whole of their private lives on display for the inspection of all in acts of consummate narcissism. Is not Steiner right, and is not part of the beauty of sexuality bound up with privacy? Remember Dussell's caress – the delicate advance and retire of mutual exploration. The word 'cynicism' comes from the Greek philosophical sect the Cynics, who got their name, 'dogs', from their insistence on showing their contempt for moral codes by having sex in public. In a hedonist society it is arguable that what pornography is principally about is pleasure – a demonstration, a celebration, perhaps even a sharing, of the pleasure of the body. As we have seen, huge sums of money are involved in this industry, and it is then part of the 'cynically consumerist present'.[35] But even when money is not the object, do not objections to 'reification' point to a falling apart of flesh and spirit, an ultimate loss of mystery about the body which is celebrated, and is this not what has to be defended?

Hearing

I turn now to my second sense, hearing. The gaze can be, we know, active, aggressive, violating. Hearing, however, is usually passive, except when we are snooping, and listening in on what we ought not to hear. Here again privacy might be the issue at stake, but that cannot provide us with the paradigm sin associated with this sense. We must turn to what it is we hear, from hearing to speaking, to the sin of the word, to what it is we intend others to hear. We could instance the torrent of noise which assails us, not only in the North, but equally in the South, where crudely erected speakers frequently drown any possibility of conversation or reflection in Third World cities and slums. But in thinking of the sin associated with hearing we need to move from the passive sense to the words we hear, to speech. For, as George Steiner says, we live 'in a culture which is, increasingly, a wind tunnel of gossip; gossip that reaches us from theology and politics to an unprecedented noising of private concerns . . . In how much of what is now pouring forth do words become word – and where is the silence needed if we are to hear that metamorphosis?' We 'speak far too much, far too easily, making common what was private, arresting into cliches of false certitude that which was provisional, personal, and therefore alive on the shadow side of speech'.[36] Here, certainly, is a sin attached to hearing. In Scripture the focus is on false witness (the ninth commandment), and on slander and malicious gossip. Given the roots of the tradition of the seven deadly sins in Scripture it is odd that these are absent from the list. 'Six things the Lord hates,' says the Book of Proverbs, 'Seven things are detestable to him:'

> A proud eye, a false tongue,
> Hands that shed innocent blood,
> A heart that forges thoughts of mischief,
> And feet that run swiftly to do evil,
> A false witness telling a pack of lies,
> And one who stirs up quarrels between brothers.
> (Prov. 6.16–19)

Sins of the word occurs three times in this list. The *Testament of Reuben*, which comes from the Hellenistic period, identifies as its seven 'spirits of deceit' promiscuity, located in the senses, insatiability, located in the stomach, strife, trickery and flattery, arrogance, lying 'which through destructiveness and rivalry handles his affairs smoothly and secretively even with his relatives and his household' and the spirit of injustice 'with which are thefts and crooked dealings'.[37] Here the word is included in six of the sins. The Christian account of the seven deadly sins received its decisive form from Gregory the Great, who was himself a disciple of Benedict. Although Benedict wrote a rule for life together, he also laid great emphasis on solitude, and the seven deadly sins we are familiar with are particularly targeted to the monk in his cell. The Jewish lists look much more to community, which lying undermines. What is destructive about lying is that it cuts away that assumption of trustworthiness on which all societies rest. Why is it that, as Henry Chadwick used to put it, 'truth telling has never stood very high on the scale of rectitude'? Some of the reasons are obvious. There is the famous example of the need to lie to someone you encounter at a crossroads waving an axe. You have just seen a terrified figure rush down the right-hand road. 'Which way did he go?' yells the axe man. 'That way,' you say, pointing down the left fork. Or there is the need to lie about Aunt Mabel's hat. 'How do you like it?' she asks. You think that you've never seen anything more frightful in your life, and that it makes her look like a scarecrow. 'Lovely,' you say. In his *Ethics*, Bonhoeffer comments on the cynicism of those people who feel that they must always tell the truth, no matter what, and who destroy human beings and human community by doing so. This is not to say that we condone lying in all circumstances, but there are clearly many so-called 'white lies' which 'do the truth', as John puts it.

Lies can destroy community, and slander can destroy an individual, but still more serious are the lies of the press, which Karl Barth spoke of as a 'gigantic maw of lying', of advertising, political rhetoric and corporate propaganda. A key contemporary example is the appropriation of the language of sustainable development by corporations whose agenda is in fact profit no matter what the price. Such language, Orwell said, is designed to make lies sound truthful and murder respectable, and to give an appearance of solidity to pure wind.[38] The point about such lying is that we must not identify it merely with tabloid journalism, or with monstrous political figures like Stalin, Hitler or Pinochet. As Karl Barth put it, 'The true and succulent lie always has something of the scent of the truth. In some manifestations of falsehood it is heavy with truth in the form of truisms, so that if we think we know and should describe it as falsehood we are bound to look like iconoclasts and must anxiously ask ourselves whether it is not we who are liars, blaspheming holy things and people . . . The instructed Grand Inquisitor or Antichrist who can commend his evil cause . . . is a sympathetic and a seriously illuminating and convincing figure.' The consummate liar 'is not against the truth but with it and for it, appealing to it with sincerity and profundity and enthusiasm'.[39] This is the first criterion of the really dangerous lie, far more of a threat in liberal democracies than in totalitarian societies where the lie is crude and palpable. Real lies are 'counterfeits which fully resemble the truth', which pushes us right back to the question of what constitutes truth in the first place.[40] We recall Van Gogh's remark, in his letters, that he wanted his paintings to lie, but to tell lies which were more truthful than the literal truth. Similarly we can think of the 'truth' of Francis Bacon's paintings, which has nothing to do with verisimilitude.

A second mark of the really dangerous lie is the question of intention. To a critic Barth once wrote: 'You say many correct things. But what is correct is not always true. Only what is kindly said is true. You do not speak a single kindly line.'[41] Behind the laborious mildness of the friends of Job, he wrote in another context, 'there is already prepared an *auto da fe* to be celebrated *ad maiorem Dei gloriam*'.[42] The purpose of the really dangerous lie is destruction, which is clearly the reason false witness figures in the commandments. False witness is the means by which we destroy an innocent person for our own ends. The slander which is condemned equally in both the Wisdom literature and the New Testament has the same intent and effect.

A third feature of the truly dangerous lie is its abstraction. Abstraction is frequently defended, and doubtless rightly, as one of the greatest human achievements, but certainly in theology, and in the pronouncements of the church above all, it can lead us to lose sight of the real human being, and thus to turn a Thou into an 'It', and this is completely to miss the substance of human truth. Think, for example, how the church has dealt, and in many instances continues to deal, with issues of divorce or homosexuality, and ask whether we do not here have examples of the pious lie.

In all these ways, as Barth reminds us, judgement begins with the house of God when it comes to lying. 'The worst of weekday lies has its roots in the even worse Sunday lie, the profane in the Christian.'[43] Here above all we can use the truth to silence the truth, or the true Witness, 'by finding for him a place, by championing him, by making him its hero, example and symbol, yet all the time patronising, interpreting, domesticating, acclimatising, accommodating, and gently but very definitely and significantly correcting him'.[44] This is a devastating possibility made all the more problematic by the fact that there are always large crowds more than ready to throw the first stone with this accusation.

Slander, false witness, the succulent lie. Are these sins of the flesh? Scarcely. In all these instances we see, as Jesus reminds us, that 'It is what comes out of a person which defiles' (Mark 7.20), drawing attention, once again, to intention. It is not so much the flesh lusting against the spirit, as the spirit corrupting the flesh.

Touch

The blessing of touch is the caress. Its curse is the blow. The earth, say the authors of Genesis, is corrupt and full of violence (Gen. 6.11). Of course, violence is not merely physical. Violence covers verbal and physical harassment, undue moral pressure, bullying, the threat of attack on the street, rape, police action, torture, terrorism, war, genocide, the Holocaust, the effects of poverty, the nuclear threat, destruction of the environment. In reflecting on the senses, however, I will concentrate on the deliberate use of touch to injure rather than to express love, and above all in torture.

Writing in 1866, Henry Lea, an American historian of torture, believed that

> In the general enlightenment which caused and accompanied the Reformation, there passed away gradually the passions which created the rigid institutions of the Middle Ages . . . In the slow evolution of the centuries it is only by comparing distant periods that we can mark our progress; but progress nevertheless exists, and future generations, perhaps, may be able to emancipate themselves wholly from the cruel and arbitary domination of superstition and force.[45]

Alas, the twentieth century, especially in its last four decades, witnessed unprecedented levels of torture. The rationale of torture is usually interrogation, which is why it is known as *la Question* in French. In fact, this has little to do with its reality, for it is, as Elaine Scarry has argued, about unmaking the world. In torture, she says, 'Each source of strength and delight, each means of moving out into the world in to oneself, becomes a means of turning the body back in on itself, forcing the body to feed on the body.' What this process does 'is to split the human being into two, to make emphatic the ever present but, except in the extremity of sickness and death, only latent distinction between self and body, between a "me" and "my body".'[46]

Earlier I remarked that the Jewish and Christian view of the human opposed any dualism of body and soul, spirit and flesh. Those philosophies which have upheld such a dualism cannot, however, be accused simply of privileging the rational and intellectual. On the contrary, they can appeal to moments of

terror or extreme alienation when people withdraw themselves from their bodies in order to distance themselves from
what is happening to them. Some accounts of prostitution
speak in the same way.

There is a paradox, which Terry Eagleton highlights, that
on the one hand 'cherished works of art' do not advocate
torture as the surest way of flourishing, and that there is an
'imposing consensus' in this regard, whilst on the other hand
the masters of suspicion – Marx, Nietzsche and Freud – all dis-
cern force at the root of meaning.[47] No philosopher or ethicist
will defend torture, but as the annual Amnesty reports make
clear, its use is so widespread it may almost be said to be the
rule rather than the exception in the contemporary world.
Huge numbers of people tortured mean huge numbers of
torturers. We know what torture does to the victim, but what
about the torturer? At the end of the Algerian conflict Père
Gilbert, a former career soldier turned Jesuit priest, said, 'I
have received enough confidences in Algeria and in France to
know into what injuries, perhaps irreparable, torture can lead
the human conscience. Many young men have "taken up the
game" and have thereby passed from mental health and
stability into terrifying states of decay, from which some will
probably never recover.'[48] And yet torture, it seems, is not just
inflicted by a handful of extremely wicked people. Stanley
Milgram's famous experiments in the 1970s, in which
participants were asked to administer increasingly high elec-
tric shocks to supposed patients, in the interests of science,
raised the question whether there is not a torturer in everyone.
Those who have researched torture suggest that it probably
creates as many sadists as it attracts. Victims of torture seem
to agree that, aside from a predictable number of constitu-
tional sadists, the torturers were people who had been
'deprived of their personalities', 'dehumanized' by being
forced to torture.[49] But is this in fact what is going on? Writing

of his torturers reporting the tortures their own comrades had undergone at the hands of Israeli forces, Brian Keenan said, 'The relish with which they spoke about torture made me think how much they secretly enjoyed reflecting on atrocities. Even as they spoke a part of them became the torturer. Without acknowledging it they were awed by the barbarity and intoxicated by its power.'[50] There is an extensive literature on what Fromm calls 'the anatomy of human destructiveness'. Distinct families of explanations trace violence to bad parenting (Alice Miller), the fractured relationships which characterize patriarchal society (Gilligan), the evolutionary need for aggression (Lorenz, Colin Morris), mimesis and scapegoating (Girard), the need to defend property (Ellacuria) and the state (Max Weber). Doubtless all of these factors have a role to play, but they say little about the ease with which states and revolutionary movements recruit torturers. Keenan's talk of intoxication is clearly part of the story. He says of Abed, the man who administered his worst beating, 'his excitement was beyond control'.[51] This kind of violence is what characterized the Viking *beserkers* and it seems to be what happens in some multiple killings. Once again we find ourselves at that 'cusp between nature and culture' where learned responses of restraint, 'biting the tongue', 'taking a deep breath' – all the disciplines of culture – are abandoned in favour of an orgy of violence. The excitement draws on the relation of power and helplessness, an absolute inversion of the care we give to infants. To have someone completely in our power can for some, and in some circumstances, invite literally devilish behaviour. Eric Fromm argues that sadistic violence is rooted in the attempt to turn impotence into omnipotence, to exercise total control. Sadism, he says, is the religion of psychical cripples.[52] On similar lines William Cavanaugh speaks of torture as a 'liturgy of omnipotence'.[53] We admire the courage of people like Keenan, but the crucial question is, what does it take not to torture, never to be drawn into that kind of vertigo?

There is some kind of answer in the New Testament, though the church's collusion with violence throughout the centuries of course calls it into question. Jesus sees that the earth is still corrupt and full of violence, that this is the land of bondage from which we need to be delivered. He analyses the causes of it in terms of domination and hierarchy, of commitment to violence as the way to revolution, as the insistence on retributive justice, as moral perfectionism. Therefore: 'It shall not be so amongst you' (Mark 10.43). He spells out an alternative way. The high road of power, wealth, legal, military or terroristic solutions – what the world calls 'strength' as Paul says – leads to disaster and the torture chamber; the low road of solidarity with the poor, giving priority to bread for my neighbour, learning to love the enemy, the discipline of forgiveness – what the world calls 'weakness' or 'folly' according to Paul – is the only road with a truly human future. Touch is a primordial gift; about the caress we can say that *natura docet*. Once we give space to its inversion, however, there is a huge and painful way back, in which the liturgy of omnipotence has to be foregone, and the liturgy of weakness and vulnerability re-learned. Touch has always been part of the Christian liturgy: in laying on of hands, in ordination, in some forms of blessing. Perhaps the kiss of peace, somewhat perfunctorily rediscovered since the Second Vatican Council, needs to be put firmly into the framework of the fragility of our ability to care, and the danger of our fantasies of omnipotence.

Taste

We come now to the two senses at the bottom of the pecking order, taste and smell. With taste we have a sense which corresponds to a sin of the flesh, gluttony, though gluttony, as a disposition, is more a vice than a sin. That gluttony is not exactly an outdated vice is shown by the statistics for obesity in Western countries, but in general it is not a vice we take seriously. Our obsession with dieting and slimming is not concerned with self-control but much more related to body image. In the classical tradition gluttony was condemned partly because all forms of pleasure were suspect, partly because it argued a weak will and partly because it actually meant a sin against the body, in making it ill.

Augustine instantiates the suspicion of pleasure. Food should be taken like medicines, he says. 'But while I pass from the discomfort of need to the tranquillity of satisfaction, the very transition contains for me an insidious trap of uncontrolled desire . . . Although health is the reason for eating and drinking, a dangerous pleasantness joins itself to the process like a companion. Many a time it tries to take first place . . . '[54] As I argued in the first chapter, such suspicion of pleasure is something we are right to put behind us, but once again we are brought back to the dialectic of nature and culture. In relation to pornography I argued that it is vital to own the complexity of human motivation, but this does not mean we can disown the notion of will. The will is about preparedness to take responsibility for what we do and who we are. Many forms of addiction therapy are actually about either strengthening or recreating the will. This is a serious issue in a society where we are urged as a public duty to give in to every impulse.

There is another more structural issue as well. In his depiction of Gluttony in *The Faerie Queen*, Spenser drew a deformed figure riding a pig:

> And like a Crane his neck was long and fyne
> With which he swallowed up excessive feast,
> for want whereof poor people often did pyne.

Sins of the flesh?

Laura Kipnis has pointed out that obesity in the United States, where one third of the population are said to be obese, increases the lower down the social scale you go; it is also possible that it is genetic.[55] On the other hand it is probable, though not statistically provable, that there was far less of it a century ago, and there is certainly far less of it in the Third World. Can the relationship between global economic disorder and the prevalence of obesity in the heartland of that disorder be factitious? In that respect gluttony, too, comes to be about power, for in a just world it would simply not be possible for that to be the case and, as Lear puts it, 'distribution should undo excess, and each man have enough' (Act IV sc. 1).

Smell

Now we come to smell, and what sin could we possibly attribute to that? Well, the Church Fathers had a ready answer. Clement of Alexandria disapproved of perfume on the grounds that it was a bait which draws us into sensual lusts. In his view, and that of many early Christians, it was a good thing to reek of 'honest' dirt and sweat.[56] Today smell remains an important social and moral indicator.

George Orwell, who was educated at Eton, famously observed that class distinction rests on the assumption that the lower classes smell. 'When we are brought up to believe that the lower classes are dirty the harm is done.'[57] Others argue that different races smell. Hitler argued that Jews smelt and that this indicated their 'moral mildew'. Some authors apply this across genders. Henry Miller had a thing about 'vaginal odour'. A whole hygiene industry has been built on the perception that 'women smell'. Conversely, a 1990 survey in Canada said women looked primarily for 'good hygiene' in men.[58]

And then again, just as part of the grace of the senses is in their evocation of memory, so this can work in the opposite direction. Here is the survivor of Auschwitz, Barbara Hyett:

> The ovens,
> the stench,
> I couldn't repeat
> the stench. You
> have to breathe.
> You can wipe out
> what you don't want
> to see. Close your
> eyes. You don't want
> to hear, don't want
> to taste. You can
> block out all the senses
> except smell.[59]

We have now run through our five senses, and I think that if we return to our opening question we will want to say that there are no specific sins of the flesh, or at least, there is no common denominator between sins particular to the various senses. I would like, however, to suggest two widely shared features. The first is that falling apart of nature and culture which we have repeatedly seen in these forms of sin. Barth speaks of this as 'dissipation', by which he means an imbalance between the ruling soul and the serving body. This is a common theme of the Christian tradition, and we find it, for example, in Jeremy Taylor, who argued that it was natural for materialists to be gluttons, 'But . . . why should we do the same things, who are led by other principles . . . who know what shall happen to a soul hereafter, and know that this time is but a passage to eternity, this body but a servant to the soul, this soul a minister to the Spirit, and the whole man in order to God and to felicity.'[60] Barth goes further arguing that a split in *either* direction, privileging either the body at the expense of the soul *or the soul at the expense of the body*, leads to a ruinous dissipation.

> As we become and are men of disorder, God necessarily becomes a stranger and enemy. For he is a God of order and peace. He is the Creator and Guarantor of the peace designed for man in his own nature as the soul of his body . . . if we choose *the flesh, ie one or other form of that dualism*, we reject God. We are blind to his work and deaf to his voice. We are no longer able to pray in any true sense. We cannot do so even if our libertinism takes a more spiritual form: perhaps a very pronounced idealism or a bold inner enthusiasm, or even an intensive religiosity, a very zealous concern for God and his cause. Born of the flesh this will always be flesh. Far from binding us to God, it will separate us from him . . . whatever form our debauchery takes, whether it is upward or downward, whether it is the libertinage of thoughts and feelings or that of the appetites, God is not there for the vagabond in us . . . The habit of self forgiveness spoils his taste for a life by free grace. Evil desire extinguishes the love of God, and therefore faith and hope in God, first in his heart, then in his thinking and action, and finally in the whole of his life. It may combine itself with the more crude or refined pretence of Christianity, but it can never go hand in hand with a true Christianity, which keeps itself in temptation and is powerful in its witness to the world.[61]

Moltmann is quite right to point out that Barth's model of 'ruling soul and serving body' is based on an idea of divine sovereignty which is insufficiently Trinitarian, and that we need to think rather of the whole human organism, the 'historical Gestalt which people, body and soul, develop in their environment'.[62] In this passage, however, Barth explicitly protests against any dualism, any splitting of nature and culture. He affirms, in fact, the need for an ongoing mutual education, within the context of the Christian tradition, which Aristotle and St Thomas spoke of as learning the virtues, and Jesus as discipleship. In this education the senses both school us and are schooled in the purposes of the kingdom.

Secondly, we saw that in many of the paradigm sins of the senses power is at the centre: in some forms of pornography, certainly, in torture, in some forms of the lie, even in gluttony. At the end of his history of Germany from 1866 to 1945, Gordon Craig remarks that 'the emphasis on power at the expense of the spirit had corrupted the values and stunted the political growth of the German people'.[63] Foucault has taught us that everyone has some power, but the problem is that some have much more than others, and in any case the question is, what we do with it. As Scottish folk singer Dick Gaughan puts it, 'What's the use of two strong arms if you only push and shove?' Power at the expense of spirit is sin, which is to say ungracious behaviour, behaviour which does not recognize our corporate rootedness in gift and therefore our common dependence. It is precisely this which Velazquez depicts in his portrait of Innocent X. This kind of power, as we see most clearly in torture, is about the unmaking of the sensed world, taking the gifts of grace and turning them into instruments of destruction. And if there is a sin against the Holy Spirit surely that is it.

If there are no sins of the flesh, what, then, is meant by bodily integrity, that situation where body and soul work together as God intended them to? At the risk of sentimental or individualist misunderstanding we might say that what bodily integrity involves is learning to love. Of course it involves 'the flesh', i.e. sex, but we need to recall Eric Fromm's insistence that love is an art and a discipline which we have to learn. It involves the intensive use of our senses, but not simply in what we call 'making love'. Much more profoundly, 'Not to be bored or boring is one of the main conditions of loving. To be active in thought, feeling, with one's eyes and ears, throughout the day, to avoid inner laziness . . . The capacity to love demands a state of intensity, awakeness, enhanced vitality, which can only be the result of a productive and active orientation in many other spheres of life.'[64] This productive and active orientation is what we can call a project. As Rowan Williams puts it, 'Decisions about our sexual lives are decisions about what we want our bodily life to say, how bodies are to be brought into the whole project of "making human sense" for ourselves and the other.'[65]

What Williams speaks of here as the project of making human sense is what Jesus speaks of as the kingdom, which takes us beyond a purely individual horizon. Love in its purely personal and physical dimensions is crucial, but it is not the kingdom. The kingdom includes justice and peace. It includes tackling the hard issues of criminal justice, of land reform, of economics, of the environment. Some years ago there was a popular film called *When Harry Met Sally*. The subtitle was: 'Can men and women just be friends or does sex always get in the way?' Predictably, the answer was that sex always got in the way, but aside from that what really irritated me about the film is that it never suggested, at any point, that there was a world out there in which people were starving and power politics being exercised. Harry and Sally went their sweet introverted ways without any knowledge of such things. To be embodied means to live somewhere, in this hut, tenement, or grand mansion; to eat this or that, bits of paper if you are poor in Rio de Janeiro, or the fruits of the whole earth if you are the fellow of an Oxford college or a North American businessman; to be unemployed and therefore unable to keep body and soul together, as we say, or to be grossing more than the poorest 17 million of your fellow citizens, as it is with the richest Mexican. Bodies are given us to challenge and change this world. To live graciously is to seek the kingdom and pursue it, and that, finally, is what we are called to use the senses for and it is failure to do so which is what we mean by that much misunderstood term 'sin', which never, I hope I have shown, refers primarily or above all to 'the flesh'.

4

The education of desire

In this chapter I turn to another classic locus of Christian thought about the senses, asceticism. From the first to the nineteenth centuries asceticism was understood as a way of disciplining the soul through the body. In the twentieth century in the West Christian ascetic disciplines collapsed, in part in the light of a much more positive attitude to the body, in part because of the seductions of consumer capitalism. I shall argue that in some respects we need to recover this tradition, specifically in relation to consumer culture.

I begin with a brief consideration of two artists who represent very different responses to the capitalist culture in which we live. Georges Grosz (1893–1959) repeatedly said of himself that he was a nihilist, and believed in nothing. Nevertheless, he struggled against his nihilism, and during the Weimar republic was the artist who most gave hope to the critics of capitalism. 'We young students did not read the newspapers in those years', said Hannah Arendt. 'Georges Grosz's cartoons seemed to us not satires but realistic reportage: we knew those types; they were all around us.'[1] His early paintings, like *Pandemonium* (1914) all depict the chaos of commercial capitalism. His cartoons depict the chaos of city life, the reduction of human beings to a mad chaos, a confusion of jumbled objects in a lurid apocalyptic world. Grosz was threatened by nihilism because he saw the nihilism at the heart of capitalist life so clearly. At the end of his life he symbolically depicted himself as 'the painter of the hole' (Plate 7), the nothingness to which modern life was reduced.

Marc Chagall (1887–1985), by contrast, born six years before Grosz, always paints out of the fullness of life of the Hebrew Scriptures, with which he was always fascinated. 'The Bible is like an echo of nature and this secret I have tried to transmit', he wrote.[2] At the age of 20 he was called back to Russia from Paris to head up the painting section in the Ministry of Culture in the new revolutionary government. Neither the failure of the revolution nor the fascism which caused him, as a Jew, to flee Europe for a time led him to cynicism or despair. Rather, all his life he painted a vision of what it meant to live in the promised land, outwith the iron cage of the capitalist economy. At the feast of Passover the minor scroll is the Song of Songs, making the point that this is what the journey to freedom is for, and this is what Chagall painted, which is why his work is so full of joy. For Chagall, eros takes us back into the Garden. He has found a way past the angel with the flaming sword. In his art he depicts the one thing needful, which has nothing to do with money. In Chagall's world nothing has a price because everything is free and for nothing. His work is a depiction of the economy of grace.

I don't think Chagall knew Luther's remark that 'The faith and the trust of the heart make both God and idol', but it would have rung a bell instantly. Talk of the heart makes us think of the individual, of our own priorities but, as we all know but nevertheless need constantly reminding, reality is *socially* constructed. None of our gods and idols are original, peculiar only to ourselves. The society, the group, the community which gives us our language, our world view, whose prejudices we imbibe without knowing or noticing, has its own gods and idols. As Luther observed, they are those things in which we really put our trust, or, as the story of the golden calf has it, the things we truly celebrate, around which we dance. The list of possible idols is a long one: nation, community, family, success, power, goods are all common. Today we have to add to this list, the body. It is a commonplace that the body has become an ersatz religion. Naomi Wolf quotes from the magazine *Positively Beautiful*: 'Stand naked in front of the full length mirror and look at yourself from the front, back and sides. Take the shades from your eyes and face the truth of the situation. Does your flesh wobble and seem dimpled? Can you see the bulges? Are your thighs very thick? Does your stomach stick out?' And she comments: 'This is self scrutiny that used to be reserved for the soul.'[3] The American cultural anthropologist Robert Murphy, writing in response to becoming crippled by a spinal tumour, wrote, 'The morality of the good body is manifest in the message pounded out daily in television commercials that "self improvement" means attaining physical fitness . . . Obesity is regarded as punishment for sloth and weak will . . . Fasting and self-inflicted physical punishment are the modern day equivalents of medieval flagellantism. They are religious rituals, part of the immortality project of a secularized middle class that no longer believes in redemption of the soul and has turned instead to redemption of the body.'[4]

The body, then, has become one of the idols we worship. I say one of the idols, for like most idolaters we are polytheists. The body cult would be inconceivable without the prevailing hedonism of Western society, the pursuit of pleasure as an end in itself. Bodies, the senses, as we saw in the first chapter, give us pleasure and are designed to do so. But neither bodies nor pleasure are intended as ends in themselves, and when they are treated as such they become idols.

Pantheons generally have a high god in the background to whom all worship really refers. It is a moot point whether this high god in our society is pleasure and the self, or whether it is consumer capitalism which, for Steven Miles, has been *the* religion of the late twentieth century.[5] Consumer capitalism possesses all the classical attributes of deity: omnipresence – saleswomen for Avon cosmetics target tribes in the Amazon; omniscience – we, and all our individual preferences, are logged on to its databases, which know to the scruple how much tea we drink and how much cheese we eat per week; and omnipotence, for 'can do' is its watchword. And in its ambitions and dreams it is infinite: it knows no limits. As a *system*, it is predicated on infinite growth, and when parts of the system – say firms, or shops – cease to expand, they die.

Are hedonism and consumerism one and the same deity after all? Miles denies that on the grounds that in the consumer society it becomes a duty on the part of the individual citizen or consumer to consume.[6] But some duties are also pleasures, which is the reason we are now urged to take 'retail therapy'. If you feel bad, go out and treat yourself. Buy something!

In any event, the body is at the centre of both hedonism and consumerism, as any walk down any high street, anywhere in the Western world, will tell you. From every window larger than life-size pictures of children, young women and young men, but especially young women, urge you not only to buy clothes, soaps, perfumes, shampoos, sportswear – items naturally associated with the body – but cars, houses, beer, wine, holidays, garden equipment, insurance – you name it. You are your body, and you need all these things to be attractive, to fit in, to be like the person in the adverts, to be truly human. Consumer capitalism exploits the body, as John O'Neill argues, by teaching us 'to disvalue it in its natural state and to revalue it only once it has been sold grace, spontaneity, vivaciousness, bounce, confidence, smoothness and freshness'.[7] It takes what is beautiful, God-given and free – all the things which Chagall paints – and uses it in the service of

Mammon, turning it into a central key in the anti-economics of consumption. It idealizes the body, so that those with bodies that don't fit the image of the adverts feel devalued, inferior. It prioritizes youth and beauty, and creates a narcissistic society of permanent adolescence. In the consumer culture, Mike Featherstone argues, lifestyle becomes critical. In this world the body becomes primarily a sign for others, and this feeds consumerism. 'The new narcissism where individuals seek to maximize and experience the range of sensations available, the search for expression and self-expression, the fascination with identity, presentation and appearance, makes the new petit-bourgeois a "natural consumer".'[8] Thus the senses are harnessed to the service of Mammon.

This system is the most powerful and the most comprehensive the world has ever known, putting all previous empires into the shade, and we owe it a great deal. It is bound up with the changes which have brought us clean water, a diet our ancestors could scarcely have dreamed of, housing which, even at its worst, would have seemed paradise to the urban poor of the 1800s, as it would to Third World slum dwellers today, rapid transport throughout the world, access to music whenever we want it, more or less instant communication, extraordinary advances in medicine, and therefore, and because of all these, greater life expectancy, and infinitely greater expectations of life. It is a cargo cult for real. As Fukuyama puts it, it succeeds because it best 'satisfies the most basic human longings'.[9] In other words, for the first time in history, he claims, human desires can be met.

To consider that claim, and as a way of getting right to the heart of the gospel, we need to ask about the nature of desire. In the New Testament we find a positive sense for desire (*epithumia*) – Jesus speaks of his desire to eat the Passover (Luke 22.15) and Paul of his desire to see his friends (1 Thess. 2.17), but the overwhelming use of the word is negative. The habit of reading Paul through Augustine's anti-Pelagian treatises has led us to think of desire primarily in terms of sexual sin. This, however, is a serious misrepresentation of the New Testament meaning. In the parable of the sower, for example, it is 'the cares of the world, the lure of wealth, and the desire for other things' which choke the word (Mark 4.19). In 1 Timothy 6.9 it again refers primarily to riches. In Colossians 3.5 it certainly means sex, but it goes beyond it, and the passage goes on to speak of anger, malice, slander and abusive language. Augustine rightly refers desire back to the tenth commandment (Ex. 20.17), but here the command not to covet applies to house (first of all) and then to the wife, the slave, the ox, donkey 'or anything that belongs to your neighbour'. As Countryman argues, property, not sex, is the key issue.[10] Coveting is about failing to respect limits, failing, in any sphere, to recognize that enough is enough. The New Testament does not try to analyse desire, but it describes how it works. In Paul's words, God hands us over to the power of our desires (Rom. 1.24). Following our desires, say the authors of James and 1 Peter, does not fulfil us but actually enslaves us. This is at the heart of the New Testament critique of desire: it is a form of addiction which destroys our freedom to serve both God and our neighbour, and may come to possess us and usurp the ultimate place in our heart which belongs to God alone.

For an analysis of desire we have to turn from the New Testament to Plato and Aristotle. Plato was much exercised by the question of desire, dealing with it at length in four of the Dialogues. In the *Philebus* he offers what is still often considered the fundamental definition of desire as a lack, an account he arrives at by considering hunger and thirst. As so often in the dialogues he uses a specious argument to come to a correct conclusion, namely that desire is not about the body but, in his terms, about the soul. I will return to that claim

86

shortly in speaking of the role of imagination. Desire is linked to pleasure, but Plato regards pleasure, the paradigm of which is eating and drinking, as 'the worst of all impostors' and certainly not the first or second thing in life. 'The first has been secured for everlasting tenure somewhere in the region of measure – of what is measured and appropriate . . . the second lies in the region of what is proportioned and beautiful, and what is perfect and satisfying.'[11]

This suspicion of pleasure is shared by the New Testament authors, where the word is only used five times, and in each case negatively. Pleasure is also one of the things which chokes the growth of the Word, and it characterizes both the person estranged from God (2 Pet. 2.13) and false teachers (2 Tim. 3.1–5).

In the *Republic* Plato argues that desire forms one of the three elements of the human soul, along with reason and *thumos*, anger, passion or high spirit. Desire is that part of the soul with which it loves, hungers, thirsts, and 'feels the flutter and titillation of other desires'.[12] Desire forms 'the mass of the soul in each of us' and is ruled by reason and *thumos* 'lest, by being filled and infected with the so-called pleasures associated with the body and so waxing big and strong, it may not keep to its own work but may undertake to enslave and rule over the classes which it is not fitting that it should, and so overturn the entire life of all'.[13] In the *Phaedrus* and the *Symposium* Plato explores the role of eros in human life, what today we would call the economy of love, in which sexual desire serves to put us on the bottom rung of the ladder which leads to love for the true, good and beautiful. Physical desire is affirmed, but, as Diotima puts it, in the *Symposium*, 'Once you have attained the very soul of beauty you will never again be seduced by the charm of gold, of dress, of comely boys, or lads just ripening to manhood.'[14] Possessed by the very soul of beauty desire takes on a different role, an eternal delight in plenitude, a self-evident, and to that extent groundless, passion for the true, good and beautiful.[15]

Beginning from the same starting point as Plato, Aristotle defines desire as 'a form of appetite'.[16] Appetite is desire for pleasure and pleasure is 'a movement of the soul by which the soul as a whole is consciously brought into its normal state'.[17] Pleasure, therefore, attends the realization of our proper human state – which it remains to define. He noted that in regard to natural appetites people only go wrong in excess,

> But with regard to the pleasures peculiar to individuals many people go wrong and in many ways. For while people who are fond of so and so are so called because they delight either in the wrong things, or more than most people do, or in the wrong way, the self indulgent exceed in all three ways.

Excess with regard to pleasures he regarded as self-indulgence and a form of childishness.[18] Such self-indulgence is at the heart of moral weakness. It is those intent on simply living rather than living well for whom desire is infinite, and who seek infinite sensual gratification.[19] The desires of the human heart are infinite, but precisely for that reason require limit. Pleasure in itself, however, Aristotle does not condemn. The paradigm case is not appetite, but that which holds our attention, like good music. True pleasures flow from worthwhile activities, and are a proper part of a truly human life.[20]

Though Augustine has a great deal to say about concupiscence, especially in the anti-Pelagian treatises, he also Christianizes the argument of the *Symposium* in the famous opening of the *Confessions*. Our deepest desire is to praise God: 'To praise you is the desire of man . . . You stir man to take pleasure in praising you, because you have made us for yourself, and our heart is restless until it rests in you.'[21] Desire is based on lack, but it is a longing for the highest good. Sensual desires are an unworthy impostor for this true form of desire. This view became fundamental for Bernard of Clairvaux and for the whole of medieval theology, which takes it for granted that God is the true object of our desire. In Aquinas's synthesis of Aristotle, Augustine and the Neo-platonism of Dionysius, the affective part of our souls is moved towards an attractive object. This movement is desire; love is our awareness of the attractiveness of the object; and the satisfying of desire is joy. Love is always characterized by a drive to union.[22] *Amor concupiscentiae*, the love of desire, is wanting good things either for oneself or for the beloved. It is inferior to *amor amicitiae*, the love of friendship, love for its own sake.[23]

Sebastian Moore puts this tradition into contemporary terms in defining desire as 'what I really want and have always wanted . . . to be more and more myself in the mystery in which I am . . . Desire is love trying to happen . . . It draws into its fulfilling meaning all the appetites of our physical being.' Agreeing with Aquinas that true desire always issues in union, he argues that its real opposite is egoism. 'It is because we do not understand desire but equate it with egoism, that we see the cross of Jesus as opposed to it. Real desire is what the cross empowers, bringing us to the death that its liberation entails. The death is the death of our present ego, whose perpetuation is the work of egoism posing as desire.'[24] The crucial thing here is the opposition between true and false desire, between egoism, locked in a monadic existence, on the one hand, and the redeemed self, celebrating relationship, on the other.

In modern times the most influential discussion of desire begins with Freud. He redefines it as libido, a term which refers to the energy of the love which strives after objects, a version of Aristotle's 'appetite'. Unlike his popularizers, Freud makes no simple equation between desire and the sex drive.

On the contrary, in what may be understood as a materialist version of the *Symposium* argument, he defines civilization as 'a process in the service of Eros, whose purpose is to combine single human individuals, and after that families, then races, peoples and nations, into one great unity, the unity of human-kind. These collections of people are to be libidinally bound to one another.'[25] Desire does not take us to the true, good and beautiful, but its job is, finally, to put an end to human conflict.

More recently Deleuze and Guattari have argued for an ontology of desire, and explicitly linked it to capitalism. They reject the characterization of desire as a lack, claiming that only a priest would maintain such a thing – a remark which puts Plato in a rather strange light. Desire is what produces, and the whole of human society is constituted by flows of desire. At one point they characterize desire as *agape*, the creative productivity of difference, the power of affirmation.[26] This sounds suspiciously like the eros with which Plato's analysis begins, only it does not include an account of the hier-archy of desire, as he did.

The point of both the Greek and the Christian traditions is that desire may be energy, but it is not undifferentiated. It requires distinctions. The distinction between real desire and desire posing as egoism is central to the critique of capitalism, which rests on a distinction between needlessly stimulated desires on the one hand and real needs on the other. It is often objected that such a distinction is unworkable because both desires and needs are socially constructed. 'The distinction is difficult to maintain', argues Brian Turner, 'because what we perceive as needs are in fact thoroughly penetrated and con-stituted by culture. The distinction between need and desire is primarily a value judgement.'[27] Case dismissed. But what did he think it was, or what does he think it ought to be? All cultures rest on value judgements, and for that matter on a distinction between desires and needs. The peculiarity of a consumerist culture is the attempt to obliterate the distinction.

Let me take the next step. Desire, in our analysis, may be defined as *imaginative work on appetite, including the appetite for knowledge*. 'Imagination', here, is what Plato refers to as the soul. It does not presuppose, as he did, a dualism between body and soul but understands human beings as bodies infused and energized by imagination. It begins, as both Plato and Aristotle did, with appetites, which accounts for the energy of desire, but it recognizes that all desire is culturally constructed, or, in my terms, is shaped by the imagination our culture makes possible. Here comes the crucial next step. All high cultures recognize that the non-divine imagination needs training and exercise. This work is called education, and this introduces *the normative dimension of desire* which Plato sets out in the *Symposium*, and Augustine in the *Confessions*. God, or the true, good and beautiful, is what desire strains towards. Education is the recognition that the imagination only flourishes when it is trained, pruned, disciplined, and that it requires goals. *All human cultures rest on an education of desire in this sense.* Jesus speaks of it as discipleship. He calls people to be disciples, which is to say to learn discipline. He is engaged in an education of desire. Plato, followed by Augustine and the whole Christian tradition, speaks of the goal of desire as 'God', but the language of the kingdom is also about the education of desire. We can learn here from E. P. Thompson's account of the utopianism of William Morris, which is not concerned with 'a moral education', but seeks 'rather, to open a way to aspiration, to "teach desire to desire, to desire better, to desire more, and *above all to desire in a different way*". Morris's Utopianism, when it succeeds, liberates desire to an uninterrupted interrogation of our values and also to its own self interrogation.'[28] To learn to desire in this interrogative way is the education we seek.

The Education of Desire

As Deleuze and Guattari recognize, capitalism itself constitutes an education of desire, namely an education to refuse limits. We can characterize it as reverse or negative education. It leads us down the ladder, not up it. It does not draw us out, but seeks to confine and limit us. The goal of desire is the true, good and beautiful or, in Christian terms, God. Christian discourse significantly alters the terms of the Platonic debate by speaking of the goal of desire, and therefore of the nature of desire, as love, and, of course, not as eros but as agape. I do not want to absolutize this distinction, but I believe it is fair to say that agape prioritizes love for the unlovable, where eros prioritizes the love which returns to me, affirms me and makes me feel good. The fragility of eros is what compels the relative distinction here, but the passion of eros remains part of agape. Any look at Bernard of Clairvaux's exposition of the *Song of Songs* shows that love, thus conceived, does not have to be passionless. On the contrary, Bernard understood God as the bridegroom, leaping across the hills in search of the beloved, the human soul. To turn from the Song of Songs to Deuteronomy, and all the prophetic writing influenced by it, we can understand God as educating and disciplining us. Desire needs education and Christianity is an alternative education of desire.

Monotheism, at least as it is understood by Judaism and Christianity, is an expression of this alternative education. It does not represent a prejudice against plurality, but rather part of the struggle for life, an insistence on ranking desires. Pantheons represent an attempt to make desires ultimate, and this, according to the prophetic analysis, destroys us. Monotheism by contrast, like the painting of Chagall, concentrates on the one thing needful.

Idols have many ways to destroy us, and one of them is to infantilize us. In *Beyond the Pleasure Principle*, Freud argued that the human infant seeks constant gratification, and falls into a rage if it cannot obtain it. Growing up is a process whereby the pleasure principle is replaced by the reality principle, in which what we do is directed by the facts of the situation, and not by gratification. The desire for gratification has to be repressed. Upon this repression is based 'all that is most precious in human civilization'.[29] What Freud calls repression here was understood by both the classical and the Christian tradition to be discipline. It is not about denying the body, but about channelling its energies creatively. The situation we are now in, however, is one where the market, which is what we call society, has to infantilize us in order to survive. In the name of 'reality' it has to move from the reality principle back to the pleasure principle, to restore pester power, to convince us that what we want we can and should have – instantly. Instant gratification is the name of the game. Eric Fromm spells out the consequences. Modern man is, he said, actually close to the picture Huxley describes in his *Brave New World*:

> well fed, well clad, satisfied sexually, yet without self, without any except the most superficial contact with his fellow men, guided by slogans which Huxley formulated so succinctly, such as: 'When the individual feels, the community reels'; or, 'Never put off till tomorrow the fun you can have today'; or as the crowning statement: 'Everybody is happy nowadays'. Man's happiness consists in 'having fun'. Having fun lies in the satisfaction of consuming and 'taking in' commodities, sights, foods, drinks, cigarettes, people, lectures, books, movies – all are consumed, swallowed. The world is one great object for our appetite, a big apple, a big bottle, a big breast; we are the sucklers, the eternally expectant ones, the hopeful ones – and the eternally disappointed ones.[30]

This infantilism is evident in the lowest common denominator culture urged on us by large sections of the media. Neil Postman, Professor of Media Studies at New York University argues, on the basis of an analysis of American television, that we are distracted by trivia. 'When cultural life is redefined as a perpetual round of entertainments,' he writes, 'when serious public conversation becomes a form of baby-talk, when, in short, a people become an audience and their public business a vaudeville act, then a nation finds itself at risk; culture death is a real possibility.' He finds Western culture in a race between education and disaster.[31] What is urged on us, even by some philosophers, is some equivalent to orgasm – pleasure, losing ourselves, gratification. To lack this gratification is to fail humanly.

In a related critique the East German Green thinker Rudolf Bahro argued that money was an expression of the subjugated ego's need for compensation. 'Because of the lack of . . . inner sovereignty people competitively accumulate power, security, comfort and armament.'[32] Money allows every little ego to conquer its world.

> The great (spiritual!) question is whether this creation of independent personality by means of the distancing effect of money was or was not an epochal substitute solution; and whether or not at least today it must be regarded as such. The bourgeois individual as a free personality is an ego still too weak to stand up to the full pressure of human contact, and needs distance for its own protection if it is to maintain its own special character, and not fall back adaptively into the 'collective', the 'natural' realm of immediate power relationships.[33]

Baalism works in our current context, I am arguing, by infantilizing us, by denying the need for a pedagogy of desire, by insisting that we stay close to the breast. It is serious because *Homo consumens* believes the gratification of desire can go on for ever and screams when trifling limitations like, for example, fuel tax, are imposed. But, as Alan Thein Durning puts it, 'If we attempt to preserve the consumer economy indefinitely, ecological forces will dismantle it savagely.'[34] It is not just a lifestyle problem but a survival problem. We cannot generalize the lifestyle of the North for six, or eight, or twelve billion human beings. We cannot even continue it for the wealthy North without irreparable damage to the earth. In this sense it is the epitome of idolatry. And the problem is that this destruction rests not on a self-evidently evil regime, like that of the Nazis, but on our normality. In Bahro's words, 'The earth can no longer put up with people as they actually are.'[35] For this reason the idolatry of consumption constitutes the critical ethical question for the foreseeable future. How to address it?

Bahro, a lifelong atheist, argued that since the problem was spiritual the solution must be spiritual also. 'No order can save us which simply limits the excesses of our greed. Only spiritual mastery of the greed itself can help us. It is perhaps only the Prophets and Buddhas, whether or not their answers were perfect, who have at least put the question radically enough.'[36] Cultures, he argued, are based on deep structures of human consciousness traditionally known as religions.[37] Given the atomization of Western cultures by capitalism, the re-establishment of a moral consciousness must 'completely constitute itself anew . . . without such a deep-level transformation, reform projects are nothing but substitute satisfaction'. This suggestion echoes the analysis of Alisdair MacIntyre's justly celebrated contention that we now live 'after virtue'. The reconstruction of consciousness or of virtue demands, said Bahro, the subordination of money, for which we need 'the most extreme exertion of consciousness, and the exercise of a spiritual quality', indeed, an ecological politics of salvation.[38]

Does this crisis provide a 'last chance for Christianity', Bahro asked ironically? I am less sceptical than he was, partly because the project of beginning 'completely anew' is self-evidently impossible. As MacIntyre insists, we can only begin with the traditions we have inherited. Amongst those traditions, I want to suggest, the Christian ascetic tradition represented an attempt to realize what Freud called the 'reality principle' as opposed to the pleasure principle, and it has much of value to offer us. Animals turn away from danger by instinct. Humans, however, 'need a conscience, social customs, cultural values and ecological wisdom to guide them'.[39] The proposal to consider the Christian ascetic tradition is a proposal to look for guidance here. Seriously? Surely the ascetic tradition was about hatred of the body, and we have only just begun, and partly with the help of Freud, to free ourselves from that. You can't seriously want to return to it – especially if you are wanting to affirm the senses? In a passionate protest Kathy Galloway writes of this tradition:

> There can be few doctrines that have been so damaging to so many, can have so defaced the image of God as one which splits the human person into parts and declares the physical intrinsically bad. Still today, lovers and counsellors, therapists and doctors are helping to pick up the pieces of lives blighted by this interpretation. It has allowed all that is sensory and feeling, all that is instinctive and intuitive to be despised, and the intellectual and 'spiritual' to be idolized. It has deprived countless men and women and children of the experience of much of what is most delightful, most hopeful and most joyful about being human. It has divided people against themselves, against each other, and against God.[40]

In support of such a view Peter Brown says of Augustine that he 'created a darkened humanism that linked the pre Christian past to the Christian present in a common distrust of sexual pleasure'.[41]

Needless to say I do not, indeed, want to return to such a tradition. But, whilst I recognize the justice of the charge, I think it has to be nuanced. In the first place, asceticism was not primarily motivated by hatred of the body. This was already true for the Colossian congregation:

> If with Christ you died to the elemental spirits of the universe why do you live as if you still belonged to the world? Why do you submit to regulations: Do not handle, do not taste, do not touch . . . These have indeed an appearance of wisdom in promoting rigour of devotion and self abasement and severity to the body, but they are of no value in checking the indulgence of the flesh. (Col. 2.20–33)

The asceticism which developed in the church did not denigrate the body but laid greater weight on it. 'Seldom, in ancient thought,' says Peter Brown, 'had the body been seen as more deeply implicated in the transformation of the soul; and never was it made to bear so heavy a burden.'[42] Ascetic thought took seriously Paul's contention that the body was the temple of the Spirit (1 Cor. 6.15). That doctrine is not uncontentious. Some contemporary writers regard it as imposing on us burdens too heavy to be borne. When children are taught their body is a temple, Nancy Mairs writes, 'I want to shout at each wide-eyed child whose body has just been snatched from her and set on a hill, remote from the grubby reality that she is hungry for lunch already with a whole hour to go . . . "Your body is a *body*. Not a holy place of worship but a person. Not a structure 'you' occupy like a maidservant in her master's house but you, yourself. Make yourself at home." '[43]

The protest is powerful, but of course holiness and grubby reality are not opposed, but go together, and what is really at stake in Paul's insistence, as the Corinthian correspondence makes clear, is *relationality*. It is just relations which make the body holy or not.

Secondly, asceticism was about solidarity with the poor. Many people in the ancient world, as indeed today, had no choice about 'ascetic' practices. They had little enough to eat as it was. The ascetic – Francis of Assisi is an obvious example – put him or herself alongside these people. Asceticism was really about what liberation theology calls the 'option for the poor'. It was the choice of voluntary poverty to put oneself alongside those enduring involuntary poverty. This call remains valid today. It is an invitation, for example, to think about our relation to the Third World over and above issues of fair trade.

Thirdly, it was a recognition, shared with all the great Greek philosphers, including Epicurus, that *virtue requires discipline and limit*. According to Cyprian, discipline is 'the guardian of all hope, the anchor cable of faith . . . the teacher of all virtue, to neglect which is certain death'.[44] We can compare Freud's argument that the role of culture is to restrain passions by collective obligations and social involvements. Anti-social behaviour is behaviour which gives satisfaction of the libido absolute priority. The reaction to 'discipline' in the wake of forty years of conscription in Europe, and a hypocritical petit-bourgeois ethic, was to be expected, but we need to find our way back to discipline as an internalized goal, which is the basis of virtue or, as Fromm would say, the ability to love. The outcome of ancient asceticism was the formation of the truly compassionate and just person. Anthony, the founder of monasticism, was, says Peter Brown, 'instantly recognizable as someone whose heart had achieved total transparency to others'.[45] That is what ascetic discipline set out to achieve.

Lastly, ascetic discipline was about genuine distinctiveness. In the second-century apologist Justin Martyr, Peter Brown points out, 'strict codes of sexual discipline were made to bear much of the weight of providing the Christian church with a distinctive code of behaviour . . . By concentrating in a single minded manner on sexual restraint and on sexual heroism, the Christians of the age of Justin had found their way to presenting themselves as the bearers of a truly universal religion. In stressing the vulnerability of all human beings to sexual desire they had been able to discover or invent a common human condition which underlay . . . complexity . . . thereby deriving simplicity out of confusion.'[46] Most contemporary writers regard the concentration on sexuality as a mistake. The real target was property, and in particular, money. The Christian ascetic tradition knew this perfectly well, as we can see by looking at the Benedictine rule, and all its precursors and followers, but this was lost sight of in the triumph of industrial capitalism in the eighteenth century, and for perfectly understandable reasons. If you have lived besieged by want, to use Flora Thompson's terms, for ever, then it is hardly surprising that new-found and seemingly infinite abundance should go to your head.[47] Today, when we see more clearly where this fifty-year binge is leading us, we are once more beginning to pick up the ancient threads.

A number of questions may be put to this proposal for reactivating the ancient ascetic tradition. The first is that it is politically infeasible. Thus Bas Wielenga argues that 'The history of Gandhism after Gandhi and of China after Mao indicates that asceticism does not provide a long term solution . . . it has no mass appeal when it comes to the economic development of society.'[48] Needless to say I am not urging asceticism on Third World societies: there we find only too much of the involuntary asceticism which voluntary asceticism exists to protest. Bas Wielenga writes from India, but writing out of New York David Korten puts the emphasis on cultural change, and in particular the movement to limit consumption in favour of simpler lifestyles. Between 12 and 15% of Americans are now said to be particpants.[49] Could it be that the hollowness of what consumerism has to offer is at last beginning to become apparent?

A second question relates to the destructiveness of a so-called Apollonian ethic of responsibility and frugality, which breeds, in Rudolf Bahro's view, exterministic accumulation and cultural cruelty. He wants an attitude which is hedonistic and friendly to the body, 'directed in Dionysian manner towards the abundance of life, corresponding to an Elysian ethic of a well disposed, happy consciousness'.[50]

But was it in fact the Apollonian attitude which led to 'exterministic accumulation and cultural cruelty'? The examples of such cruelty which spring to mind are the conquest of South America, the slave trade and the competition between European nations which was responsible for two world wars. In each case Apollonian attitudes were hardly the problem. Equally we can ask whether the Elysian ethic is anything but a Rousseauesqe fantasy. At the same time Bahro is asking, along with eco-feminists like Vandana Shiva and Maria Mies, and with American critics of capitalism like David Korten or Wendell Berry, for cultural change. Such change, they agree, is the indispensable prelude to political change. In a body culture like that of the contemporary West this involves a change of attitude to the body. Serving God is the way to find out how to liberate our truest and deepest desires, says the Christian tradition, but this liberation involves an ongoing education of the senses. What is needed is a movement for the liberation of all forms of desire, including eros, from the tyranny of consumerism.[51]

We have to find ways of living which protest the commodification of the body whilst honouring what the creator has given us. Given the twin imperatives of saving our planet and seeing that resources are justly distributed amongst the world's population, I would say that what we need is a body-friendly asceticism, which is about harnessing desire to the purposes of the kingdom. William Countryman says that the measure of sexuality that accords with the New Testament is simply this: 'The degree to which it rejoices in the whole creation, in what is given to others as well as to each of us, while enabling us always to leave the final word to God, who is the beginning and end of all things.'[52] Such rejoicing in the whole creation does not preclude but rather demands the kind of asceticism I am arguing for. Bahro seems to affirm this kind of asceticism, for he argues that the only possibility of survival is the adoption of a lifestyle of 'voluntary simplicity and frugal beauty based on a subsistence economy – and then only if we limit our numbers'.[53] For this reason, 'The market *must* be limited to really necessary exchanges beyond the locality. We *must* ration what we eat and consume, and we *must* limit our numbers. This is not a call for regulation "starting tomorrow morning", but a demand that we recognise a principle.'[54] Bahro speaks as a secular rationalist who sees the importance of religious traditions. Vandana Shiva speaks as a Hindu who finds resources for life within her tradition. Korten calls for cultural change by appealing to the informed conscience. It is not a question of a 'last chance for Christianity' but it is a question of whether Christianity, so deeply involved in early colonialism, which Vandana Shiva identifies as the first phase of globalization, has anything to contribute. I have tried to argue that what we have to recover is an understanding of discipleship as a real discipline. For years, now, the Church has emphasized the importance of stewardship. Much more radically it needs to be concerned with the emergence of what Bahro calls 'a new, just, money order based on small property', for, 'it is not monopolistic big capital, always so easy to condemn, which merits our attention, but money, the daily small change. For it is by this we are bound.' 'Money is the universal drug with which we multiply our tendency to overthrow the balance of nature. For this reason an economic society with the moneymaking drive at its core cannot be saved. It doesn't permit any independent ordering to arise, because it itself dominates the entire field.'[55] Jesus expressed this aphoristically in saying that you cannot serve both God and Mammon.

In these imperatives the personal is the political. If cultural change is at the heart of the matter then it is clear that 'All of us can indeed take small steps in the alternative direction and become progressively involved in the struggle for eco justice, inspired by the hope and conviction that spaces will open up for the radical reorientation and transformation which is needed.'[56] At the same time movements are needed, for education is never a solitary process. In the final chapter I wish to ask how such a movement might occur, and such an education of desire be forwarded, within the Christian context.

5

Celebrating bodies

Taking up an Augustinian theme, Rudolf Bahro looks, for the cultural and political change we need, to the formation of a new spiritual authority, an Invisible Church, which stands open to all, and to which all belong 'with that part of their consciousness which is free for the new world'. It exists, he says, 'as a horizontal, multilateral network. It forbids itself all direct or indirect constitution as a commanding social or political power. The eco-spiritual movement does not aim at immediate success, nor at a numerical growth, but builds on the radiation of everything which is true to life, biophile, loving, done with total commitment, which arises in it.'[1] This sounds too like the ephemeral hippiedom of the late 1960s and early 1970s to be comfortable. The growth of church structures in the first and second centuries was not just a fall from primitive innocence, but occurred precisely because the idea of spontaneous radiation does not take adequate account, not only of powers of co-option, but of the sheer fragility of human relationships and communities, which Bahro tragically experienced in his own life. What is going on in the church at the moment is a profound move beyond present structural boundaries, but we will, I believe, continue to need the structures at least in some shape or form. The church exists, said Augsburg, where the gospel is preached (*docetur*) and the sacraments rightly administered (Article 7). The church exists, we may say, where human desire is educated, disciplined, by Word and sacrament.

In the Christian tradition it is above all the eucharist which exists to do this disciplinary and educative work. Standing at the heart of Christian education it is a sign act in which a sign we call 'body' mediates between the historical memory of the physical body of Christ, tortured to death, and the body of believers called to become an alternative community, a new inclusive body which challenges the bodily disciplines of capitalism. The body, we have seen, becomes a consuming body and itself an object of consumption. The eucharist, by contrast, is a call to reverent consumption not for its own sake, but for the sake of the poor, to enable reverent consumption on their part, and for the sake of God's beautiful earth, God's gift to us. The eucharist has been understood as a school of the senses at least since Irenaeus in the second century. In the Catholic tradition the senses have been celebrated through music, the use of incense, vestments, candles and liturgical symbols. The eucharist affirms the body, but in the context of the kingdom. This kingdom reference means that in every culture and every context it is always a sign act of both affirmation and denial. In the context of the consumer capitalism in which we live it has to be both affirmative of the physical body, and of the earth, and *for that very reason* hostile to all forms of consumerism. For us the eucharist has to function, as it was intended to, as a school of just and equal sharing, a school in which we recall the exploitation of bodies and look forward to a situation beyond exploitation. As a school of celebration it teaches us hope, but as a school of asceticism it teaches us resistance. In both it is a glorious affirmation of the senses which God has gifted us, through which we gift ourselves to each other, through which we celebrate our creator, and through which our creator celebrates us.

I am not arguing that the eucharist is the *raison d'être* of Christian life, but I do see it as at the heart of the Christian education of desire. To illustrate this we can consider the story Vereene Parnell tells, of how Redeemer Church in Morristown, USA, a congregation which was respectably dying, 'huddled around liturgical half-measures in a cold stone building waiting for the last candle to burn out', was revitalized by engagement with AIDS.[2] The son of a couple in the small congregation developed AIDS, and the congregation at once rallied round though visits, providing food, and letters of love and support. As the father noted, this was nothing surprising: 'It's what churches do.' Following the son's death, sympathy, support and solidarity turned to active engagement with the wider issue. The rectory was turned into transitional housing for individuals and families left homeless because of HIV/AIDS. Through this activity the church was reborn, and the liturgy, the eucharist, became its corporate heartbeat, a school for attention to corporeality, a school for corporate accountability. 'Far from fostering complacency or nostalgia,' writes Parnell, 'ritual participation in past victories – and defeat – becomes "dangerous" in a radically redemptive sense when, and only when, it fuels continuing resistance to and transformation of institutions and ideologies of oppression.

> The liturgies that resurrect and reincarnate such stories speak a new world into being. They are . . . 'eschatological acts bringing about the reality they describe' . . . Through such eschatological acts [this church] has, de facto, resurrected the eucharistic concept of 'transubstantiation'. No longer at issue – for most communicants – is the transformation of bread and wine into flesh and blood, rather the substantial transformation of the very incarnate body of Christ, the Church, through sharing the ritual meal at the altar, on the soup kitchen line . . . in members' homes or hospital waiting rooms. The bodies of Christ multiply like loaves and fishes, becoming flesh and blood, creative spirit,

beating heart, a community of extraordinary and everyday saints once more.'[3]

There's no answer to the riddle of chicken and egg. We all know what the liberation theologians have been teaching us for more than thirty years, that theology is a second step. And by the same token, liturgy is most certainly a second step. But it's the second step in the tango. You take a first step, then you take a second step. If you don't, you fall over.

The first step is action. Redeemer Church came back to life when it took risks, got involved in AIDS, welcomed the homosexual community and people with AIDS into its ranks.

But of course this was not quite a first step, it was more the rejuvenation of an ailing and arthritic body. There was a heartbeat there – the compassion and down to earth goodness that knew that if one of the congregation had AIDS then you supported them and their family. That was the spark which became the flame. And that heartbeat was sustained over decades in what seemed to be a moribund church by the reading of the Word and by an institutionalized liturgy. We do our very best to quench the Spirit by our church practices, but somehow we don't quite succeed. So perhaps what we ought to say is that action, involvement, engagement is what galvanized the church into life once more. Galvanized into life it needed food. The old liturgies no longer fed it. It needed new, vibrant liturgies, new songs, new ways of hearing the Word. These new liturgies fed new patterns of engagement. The hermeneutic spiral had begun.

Going to church these days can often be a depressing experience. Occasionally one encounters congregations which, like Redeemer Church, have been galvanized into life, but more often they seem to be in a persistent vegetative state. If so, engagement and risk around some vital issue – it may be AIDS, it may be asylum seekers, it may be nuclear weapons, it may be the homeless or other marginalized groups, it may be the global economy – seems to be the cure. Liturgical reform cannot be the cure, of that I am convinced. You cannot begin there without ending up with narcissism and aestheticism, a liturgy which may be very 'beautiful' but precious, and in which therefore there is no life blood. Liturgy has to be a second step, but it's a second step we cannot do without. If, as I have claimed, the global economy, of which the fetishization of the body is an important part, is one of the key ethical issues we face, then we need to see how the eucharist bears on it.

The 'global economy' can seem remote and abstract as an issue until we start looking at the labels on our clothes, and the 'Country of Origin' tags in our supermarkets. The global economy, in fact, is part of the fabric of our daily lives. A cursory check at the local supermarket reveals that our beans come from Kenya, our apples from South Africa, our oranges from Morocco or Israel, our avocados from Chile, our soya from Brazil, our butter from Denmark, our wine, and sometimes even our beer, from Australia or the United States, our sardines from Portugal, and so on and so forth. Well so what? It's good to acknowledge our mutual dependence. Except that that is not what we are doing. What we are doing is enriching, and strengthening the power of, the big corporations, impoverishing the poor countries, and destroying the environment. I want, then, to make four connections between the global economy and our celebration of eucharist.

First, the global economy is wedded to growth. Bigger is not just better, it is essential. As a *system*, the global economy is predicated on infinite growth, and when parts of the system – say firms, or shops – cease to expand, they die. Top executives from the big corporations have confessed how, when *Limits to Growth* came out in 1972, and *Small is Beautiful* the following year, a shiver ran down corporate spines. They saw a truly dangerous enemy, and they acted to counter it. The notion that there is any need to limit growth has been rubbished time and again in the house magazines of corporate capital – journals like *The Economist* – and by numerous professional economists. It's all a big mistake, a pathetic fallacy on the part of bleeding heart vegetarian sandal wearing do gooders. This rhetoric is shriller now than ever, and the reason is that that claim is wearing a bit thin. In 1972 the *Limits to Growth* team thought oil would be the problem, but oil is not the problem. Water, grain, and fish – the things which maintain life at the most basic level – are the problem. Since 1972 world population has increased hugely to its present state of over 6 billion. All over the world these populations put increasing pressure on water. The Gulf war was over oil, but already the 1966 war between Israel and Syria was over who controls the head waters of the Jordan. Water wars are increasingly the shape of the future. Profligate use of aquifer resources in places like Saudi Arabia and Texas means that resources which have lain untapped for hundreds of thousands of years, and which will take as long to replenish, have been exhausted in decades. Lester Brown, of the World Watch Institute, argues that the world's farmers face a steady shrinkage in grainland and water irrigation per person. In any case 10 to 15 acres of fertile land are required to maintain consumption of the average person in a high income country. A decade ago only 4 acres per person was left. It has shrunk dramatically since then. There is simply not enough land left to support our lifestyle. Meanwhile all over the world fisheries are collapsing, first on the Aral Sea, then in India, then in Europe and North America. The reason? Highly mechanized trawlers take too much too quickly to allow fish stocks to regenerate.

How does the eucharist bear on this? It is essential to understand that the eucharist did not originate just in the so-called

'Last Supper'. That idea has been drummed into us over so many centuries, principally by the role of the Last Supper narratives in our liturgy, that it has become a subconscious assumption. But the eucharist is rooted in the whole life practice of Jesus, and amongst other things in what we call the great feedings, which all the Gospels record, and the synoptics record twice. And again, these events have been trivialized by being treated as a miraculous multiplication of particles. But they are not that. They represent the triumph of an economy of sharing over an economy of greed. Greed is not just about wanting to finish the whole of my chocolate bar before someone I know turns up and I am shamed into sharing it. It's not just about the rich or the very rich constantly wanting more, like the Augsburg banker Jacob Fugger, the richest man of his day who, when asked if he could imagine ever having enough, said he could never imagine such a time. At its root it's about that turned-in attitude which isn't open to the neighbour. Its root may very well be in fear, for we are told that evolution programmes us to eat as much as we can when we can, because for most of human history it would not be clear where our next meal was coming from. Jesus addresses this deep-seated fear in the miracles of feeding.

According to the stories, Jesus has been preaching all day, and the disciples come to him and say: 'Enough sermonizing! So we don't live by bread alone, but we can't live without it either. We've got to feed these people! What are you going to do about it?' Philip adds, 'You've got a real problem on your hands, Jesus. You need six months' wages to feed this lot.' So Jesus says, 'OK, get everyone to sit down.' 'Now – let's see what we've got. Who's got some food we could share?' Everyone keeps silent because they know that if they share the cheese sandwich they brought with them they'll end up with a minute crumb, and they don't want to walk home with an empty belly. So there's silence. 'Anyone got any food?' hollers

Peter. And a child, who hasn't learned to calculate yet, says –
'Here. You can have my lunch packet – I've got some sardines
and a couple of bread rolls.' 'OK,' says Jesus, 'share them
round.' And at that, everyone is shamed into sharing. And
what happens? There's more than enough – food to spare.
Mahatma Gandhi's famous remark that there was enough for
everyone's need but not for everyone's greed is a perfect
summary of the outcome of the story.

The eucharist comes out of the great feedings: it is a sign act
about the need to share what we have. But if we don't share
what we have, it becomes an empty sign. To become a burning sign it needs to be related to action.

And there is more to it than that. Every detail of the Gospel
narratives relates in some way or other to the stories of the
Hebrew Bible, and especially to the story of Israel's liberation
from Egypt and to what happened thereafter, the long journey
through the desert, accompanied by constant loss of hope. In
this case the feeding in the wilderness clearly takes us to
Numbers 11, which picks up the story at the moment when
hunger has at last really begun to bite. Here is a rough para-
phrase of verses 4–6:

> Those who read the Murdoch press among them
> (*asaphsuph* – a hapax legomenon in the Hebrew Bible) had
> a strong craving; and the Israelites wept again, and said,
> 'If only we could get back to the Tesco's in Luxor. We
> remember the fish we used to eat in Egypt for nothing, the
> cucumbers, the melons, the leeks, the onions, and the
> garlic; but now our strength is dried up, and there is
> nothing at all but this so-called 'food for revolutionaries',
> aka manna, to look at. (Num. 11.4–6)

We are misled by our hymns. We come to think of manna as
something delicious – a bit like halva – but the stories make

clear that it wasn't. It was hard tack – survival rations. Day after day it was extremely boring. Moreover, it had a built-in anti-greed principle. If you tried to store it, or hoard it, it went rotten.

The Authorized Version of the Bible translates *asaphsuph* as 'mixed multitude'. The Revised Standard Version translates it as 'the rabble'. But the *asaphsuph* is the mass of believers from Moses to the present. YHWH says: 'I'm going to lead you to freedom.' We say 'Great.' Ten days on the road we're saying: 'When can we go home? We don't want freedom at the cost of comfort and security.' YHWH says: 'I'll give you manna.' 'Great,' we say. After a week we're saying: 'Oh my God, not manna again. Look YHWH, didn't you ever go to Tesco's?' Where the Numbers story says 'manna', Jesus puts the bread of sharing. 'Great,' we say. And for a while it gives us quite a buzz. But nobody else does it. And we're missing out. We want our share of this world's goods. Come on! We're not ascetics. Give us a break!

John reflects on both of these stories together. After the feeding Jesus crosses the sea of Galilee and the crowd ask him about the meaning of the sign.

> Our ancestors ate the manna in the wilderness; as it is written, 'He gave them bread from heaven to eat.' Then Jesus said to them, 'Truly I tell you, it was not Moses who gave you the bread from heaven, but it is my Father who gives you the true bread from heaven. For the bread of God is that which comes down from heaven and gives life to the world. They said to him, 'Sir, give us this bread always.' Jesus said to them, 'I am the bread of life. Whoever comes to me will never be hungry; and whoever believes in me will never be thirsty.' (John 6.31–5)

At the end of the feeding story in John, the disciples gather up the crumbs from the bread rolls and they fill twelve baskets. John comments: 'When the people saw the sign that had been done, they began to say, 'This is indeed the prophet who is to come into the world.' In other words: When the people saw the triumph of an economy of sharing over an economy of greed, when they saw someone who could teach people the basic meaning of Torah so that justice was done and people were filled, and Torah became as it was supposed to, bread of life, just as it was promised in Deuteronomy 6, then they began to say – 'Maybe this *is* the prophet Deuteronomy talked about' (Deut. 18.15). 'I am the bread of life,' says Jesus. He is the bread of life because he lives God's Word, or as John prefers to say, embodies it. As a good Jew, John says: Torah, God's Word, God's Law, was in the beginning with God. That Word took flesh in Jesus. In his Gospel John has a whole series of signs to show us that Jesus does in fact embody that Word. Water becomes wine at a marriage banquet. Why? Because the Song of Songs is the minor scroll read at the feast of Passover. That's what marks the Gospel off from the old form of Marxism-Leninism, with all those awful statues of heroic workers striving into the future. Revolutionary struggle is not the be all and end all, said the Rabbis. We have a revolution so that we are free to make love, and so that our children can grow up in peace and security. Love is the purpose of the revolution. So Jesus sanctifies the purpose of the revolution. He consecrates the celebration. The miracle at Cana in Galilee is about the *Buena Vista Social Club*.[4] Near the beginning of the film, the camera pans round the streets and walls of Havana. 'This revolution lasts for ever,' say the slogans on the walls. Of course, it doesn't. It's doomed, just as the Sandinista victory in Nicaragua was doomed, just as the original Christian revolution was doomed by Constantine and Gregory the Great. But that's not the point. The revolution, the journey through the wilderness, goes on. *This* revolution lives for ever. We have to live on boring old manna a lot of the time. But don't forget what the revolution is for. That's why John calls Cana 'the beginning of signs'. Then Jesus heals a man born blind, which is a Messianic sign, a sign that the Messiah has arrived. Why? Because seeing the point, seeing through the lies and evasions of the propaganda and the press, whether of Nero or BP or Shell, Cargill or Monsanto, is always profoundly difficult. More than that, it's a miracle that we ever get to the truth. 'I am the Light', says Jesus, meaning that he enables us to see through the subterfuges which the world, what John calls the world, which means Whitehall, and Washington and all that, deceives us with. Jesus raises Lazarus from the dead. When he comes to his tomb he says, 'Unbind him and let him go.' Looking round, John sees people in the tomb of hopelessness and despair in the face of the all-encompassing Roman empire, in face of the all-encompassing empire of the World Bank and the IMF, and the global corporations. And he says, Jesus can raise you from that death in life. He can unbind you and let you go, let you go into history, to change it, to effect that revolution which never ends. He does so because he really puts his trust in God's Word, Torah; he makes that Word flesh. 'Are you a king because you compete in cedar?' asks Jeremiah of king Shallum:

> Did not your father eat and drink
> and do justice and righteousness?
> He judged the cause of the poor and needy;
> then it was well.
> Is not this to know me, says YHWH. (Jer. 22.15–16)

Jesus is the bread of life because he embodies, lives out – incarnates is the Latin word – that Word. He eats and drinks and does justice and righteousness. He invites us to do the same. Liturgiologists tell us that at the heart of the eucharist is the *anamnesis* – the recalling. Well, that is what we recall, that God's word of justice and peace for the nations was embodied in Jesus and calls us in our turn to live that embodiment in our own time and to the limits of our power.

A second connection between the eucharist and the global economy comes in relation to 'the environment', by which I mean, first, pollution, environmental degradation and the loss of biodiversity and, second, the macro problems like the destruction of the ozone layer and global warming. These are also linked to the global economy and consumer capitalism and therefore also to the eucharist.

We all know a bit about global warming by now because of its impact on our weather. Global warming is bringing about potentially catastrophic changes in the earth's climate with huge implications for millions of people living on shorelines and a devastating impact on crop management. The major cause of global warming is carbon dioxide emissions. The world's consumer class is responsible for an estimated two-thirds of carbon dioxide emissions each year. The poor release one-tenth of a ton each year; the middle income group half a ton; the consumer class three and a half tons; the richest tenth of Americans 11 tons. You can calculate fossil fuel allowances per person for 6 billion, given the capacity of global 'sinks' – the inbuilt mechanisms for dealing with potentially toxic wastes. The average family car covering 11,000 miles burns two persons' fuel allowance, and heating an average British house burns four persons' fuel allowance. Flying from Europe to North America uses two persons' fuel allowance. Stand in any airport and look at the volume of traffic and ask whether the realization of the need to respect global 'sinks' has begun to be appreciated.

In terms of pollution, we also all know about Chernobyl, the effects of which are still with us, and will be for millennia.

Celebrating bodies

What we are less conscious of is the ever increasing amount of hazardous waste, 303 billion tons ten years ago, produced by the world's rich countries. We still have not found effective ways of dealing with this, and we have the spectacle of tankers loaded with lethal waste limping from port to port around the world. The amount grows as the economy expands.

The link of environmental degradation to the economy can be clearly seen by the fact that it is the world's most indebted countries – Brazil, Mexico, Zaire, Bolivia, Indonesia and Malaysia – which are responsible for half of the tropical forest lost between 1991 and 1995. And this destruction goes on apace. It is a form of consumption. Once upon a time we were *Homo sapiens*; Huizinga argued we were *Homo ludens*; today, however, we are *Homo consumens*. We are always described as consumers these days, and the description is well chosen. Deuteronomy sets two ways before us, a way of obedience and blessing and a way of disobedience and death. If we choose the latter, then, the Deuteronomic authors say, plagues and enemies will consume our livestock, crops and trees, 'leaving you neither grain, wine and oil nor the increase of your cattle until you perish' (Deut. 28.51). The consumer economy is not just a lifestyle problem but a survival problem.

Another, rather old fashioned, use of the verb 'to consume' relates to the eucharist. If there are elements left over, the liturgical rubrics tell us, and we are not going to reserve them, then we must 'consume them reverently'. That idea of reverent consumption is something we would do well to recover. At the so-called Last Supper, the stories tell us, Jesus broke bread and blessed it. What was this blessing? It was, of course, giving thanks over it. Blessing did not mean waving your hand over an object, say a piece of bread, and doing something to it. It meant praising the creator, who had given it. We now incorporate this blessing into the eucharist:

Blessed are you, Lord of the universe, through whom we have this bread to offer.

It was at the moment of the blessing that the disciples at Emmaus recognized Jesus, which probably means it was a highly characteristic action of his. He liked to bless, and give thanks to God, because that was the absolutely fundamental predisposition of the texts of his people. They breathe thankfulness, dependence, gratitude. Gratitude follows grace, says Karl Barth, as thunder follows lightning. Because what we receive is gift, grace, we have to be thankful for it. Personally, I think that as Christian people it's vital that we recover the practice of grace before meals – before every meal – as an inner protest against irreverent, which is to say planet-destroying, consumption. But alongside that, the eucharist is also intended as a school of gratitude, teaching us to value God's creation, to treat it with respect and gratitude and not to despise it.

A third connection between our economy and the multiple bodies of the eucharist can be found in world terms of trade. We are constantly told by those in charge that things are getting better. What this is supposed to mean is that more and more people are getting more and more of an expanding pie. Unfortunately this is a lie. The 1997 United Nations Development Report noted that 'The share of the poorest 20 per cent of the world's people in global income now stands at a miserable 1.1 per cent, down from 1.4 per cent in 1991 and 2.3 per cent in 1960. It continues to shrink.' And it has continued to shrink. In 1999 at the G7 summit the rich nations promised to write off $45 billion worth of debt. Till today, nothing has been done. Today, and every day, India services a debt burden of more than £7 million to international financial institutions. In Brazil more than £30 billion has to be paid in 2000 in debt-servicing. And when we talk about debt remission they talk about moral hazard. It's a joke invented in hell.

The very first record of the eucharist we have comes from Paul's problems with the congregation in Corinth, who were split between rich and poor. Paul lays into the rich members of the congregation because they eat without regard for their poor members. When the rich overeat, and the poor have to go hungry, he says, this dishonours the church of God – it can't be eucharist (1 Cor. 11.20). It is in this situation he rehearses the tradition of what we call the Last Supper. Then he says: those who eat and drink in this way – ignoring differences between rich and poor – will be answerable for the body and blood of the Lord. Those who eat and drink without discerning the body – that body which is made up by all believers – eat and drink judgement against themselves (1 Cor. 11.29).

Behind this passage lies Deuteronomy 15, the section of Deuteronomy which deals with Jubilee. Deuteronomy orders a remission of debt every seventh year, and says that if that is followed, 'there will be no poor amongst you' (Deut. 15.4). This is the passage Jesus alludes to in the story of the anointing at Bethany (Matt. 26.6 ff.; Mark 14.3 ff.; John 12.1 ff.) which is so often misunderstood. Some of the disciples say: This could have been sold and given to Oxfam. Jesus says: If you remember what is said in Deuteronomy, and if Torah was followed, there would be no poor amongst you.

Paul, too, has it in mind. The eucharist, he says, is the instantiation of this Jubilee legislation, which, by remission of debt, sees that there will be no poor amongst you. If you maintain and even increase such divisions, then you turn eucharist into its opposite, and simply bring judgement on yourselves. From the word go, when we first encounter the eucharist in the church, therefore, there is a direct link between debt remission, the elimination of poverty, and celebration of eucharist.

Finally, my fourth connection between the eucharist and the global economy: this economy takes the form of a competitive power contest, the kind of contest our education system is today designed to train us for. We are all familiar with the debt problem through Jubilee 2000, but debt is only the tip of the iceberg. Trade is more serious still. The doctrine of free trade is the mantra of United States-led capitalism, but in fact, no country has more protectionist legislation than that country, and it pursues its own advantage in the market place savagely. The Multi Fibre Arrangement (MFA), which protects Europe and America against cheap imports from the South, is in force till 2005, and what's the betting it will then be renewed? The overall cost of the MFA to developing countries is estimated at about \$50 billion a year, roughly equal to the total of development aid. The EU specifically excludes metals, agricultural products and textiles from free trade schemes. Discrimination against basic commodities remains the biggest weapon against the poor countries, even more serious than debt.

Forty per cent of world trade is in the hands of the top 350 companies. The largest 10 corporations control assets which represent three times the total income of the world's poorest 38 countries. Of the world's 100 largest economies, 50 are transnational corporations. The 48 least developed countries account for less than 0.3% of world trade. Real commodity prices were 45% lower in the 1990s than in the 1980s. The Multilateral Agreement on Investment, defended passionately by Britain's Labour government, was intended to give companies power over democratically elected governments – except those in the United States, which had all voted opt-out clauses. For the moment it has been stalled, but it will certainly be back.

Another aspect of the dominance of the global economy by the transnationals is the attempt to patent, and make money out of, life, a process Vandana Shiva has dubbed 'biopiracy'. For example, US and Japanese firms have taken out patents on neem-based solutions which have been used in India for millennia. When Monsanto marketed (a disastrously unsuccessful) cotton seed it notified farmers that 'Saving or selling the seed for replanting will violate the limited license and infringe upon the patent rights of Monsanto. This may subject you to prosecution under federal law.'[5] As Brewster Kneen puts it, 'Genetic engineering is an expression of ingratitude and disrespect, if not contempt. It is a vehicle, in practice, of an attitude of domination and ownership, as expressed in the assumption that it is possible, reasonable, and morally acceptable to claim ownership over life. The claim that it is possible to own life, at least to the extent of being able to claim a patent on a life process or life form, is so outrageous socially and ethically as to be hardly worth debating.'[6] Not, however, to corporate lawyers.

After the blessing and the breaking at the so-called Last Supper come the famous words, 'Do this, in remembrance of me.' Do what in remembrance of me? For centuries it has been assumed that it is the repetition of a set of liturgical actions but, given Jesus' practice in the Gospels, that seems highly unlikely. He wasn't a person wedded to rituals, except for the small intimate human ones of welcoming children, seeing that people get fed, caring for the sick.

The command to 'do this' seems to relate much more to Jesus giving his life for others, and so 'do this' means, 'Let the breaking and the sharing of your continued table fellowship remind you of how my life was broken and poured out for others, and may you do likewise.' And this is in fact how people like Augustine understood the eucharistic sacrifice. It is part of Jesus' project of constructing an alternative society. This way of understanding it is in line with the account of the Last Supper we have in John. According to John Jesus gets up from table, girds himself with a towel, and performs the action of a slave, washing his disciples' feet. Reflecting on such stories Paul writes: 'Let the same mind be in you as was in Christ Jesus, who because he was in the form of God, did not regard equality with God as something to be exploited, but emptied himself, taking the form of a slave' (Phil. 2.6). The translations always say, 'although he was in the form of God', subconsciously presupposing the managerial gods of paganism, with their six-figure salaries. But Paul, like Jesus before him, thinks rather of the God of Israel, who serves Israel, becomes a slave for them. To have the mind of Christ is to adopt this alternative lifestyle. William Cavanaugh argues that the Church's resistance to the regime of torture 'depends on its ability to constitute itself as a disciplined social body capable of countering the discipline of the State'.

> Liturgy and sacraments are disciplines of bodies and souls which help form people into the habits, or virtues, necessary to perform the Gospel imperative to take up one's cross and follow Christ. In the contest over bodies, both individual and social, Christian resistance will depend on having a visible body, ie a counter discipline and a counter performance.[7]

He writes in the context of torture. Let's put his argument in the context of a consumer economy, and a world structured round great corporations, now blasphemously proclaiming themselves to be 'servants'. Jesus said to his disciples: 'It shall not be so amongst you.' This word, in Mark 10.43, is a fundamental counter-cultural text. We are called to resist these destructive practices of power, and to envisage and to practise the economy of reverent consumption, the economy of service. Big business tells us that only the way of power makes sense, that big is beautiful. The story of the trek through the desert includes an encounter with the managers of the big corporations, and the editors of the financial papers, and the politicians and the neo-liberal economists. Moses sends out his scouts, and they come back with beautiful bunches of grapes, but also scared to death:

> We came to the land to which you sent us; it flows with milk and honey, and this is its fruit. Yet the people who live in the land are strong, and the towns are fortified and large; and besides we saw the descendants of Anak there . . . to ourselves we seemed like grasshoppers, and so seemed we to them. (Num. 13.27)

Things don't change, do they? We peek at the people who occupy the promised land, with their armies, and their lawyers, and their ownership of the press, and their business success, and all their money, and we say: 'Let's go back to Egypt.'

The descendants of Anak tell us that power and success is the only way because that is how people are made. But excuse me, when it comes to how people are made, it is not for them to lay down the law. I don't find Social Darwinism in the New Testament. Perhaps I don't find the altruistic gene there either, but I do find the view that only by renouncing power and learning to serve do we find our full humanness. Can that become an economic principle? Of course it can. The word for it is cooperation. Economists faint at the term not because it is impossible but because it means the end of hierarchy, power structures, managerial salaries. In this ongoing argument things are changing. At the moment the latest manifestation of capitalism, finance capitalism, is at its acme. But the bottom line is, it's unsustainable. We have to find another way of doing things. World leaders are fond of telling us there is 'no alternative'. They are right, though not in the sense they intend. And so we'd better start learning, and in our imagining we can nourish ourselves by returning to the eucharist.

The church's task varies according to its context. In the eighteenth century, when the poor were drowning themselves in gin, it might be right to insist on being teetotal. Today the equivalent of gin is consumption. In countering that, the eucharist, affirming the body and therefore protesting every attempt to colonize, patent and exploit it, stands at the centre of Christian life. In the eucharist the Word of justice which becomes the bread of life for us in Christ is given us as manna – nothing more; bread for our revolutionary journey; bread for a new world; bread for the poor. This, finally, is what manna is – Word and sacrament, food for our journey. I have several times used the phrase, the 'so-called Last Supper'. And the reason is, of course, that Jesus broke bread with the disciples at Emmaus, and by the lakeside. The fixation on what happened before Gethsemane and Calvary concentrates on the cross at the expense of resurrection. But of course, they interpret each other. Only because there was Emmaus is the eucharist a sign of hope. In Luke's story the disciples stay in Jerusalem until Pentecost, and only then are they slowly scattered to the ends of the earth. In Matthew it happens at the resurrection itself. These stories too have their Old Testament analogue. They recall the conclusion of the story about the manna. It reads: 'And the people of Israel journeyed on' (Num. 11.35).

Notes

1. Instruments of grace

1. *Constable's 'English Landscape Scenery'*, ed. A. Wilton, British Museum Publications 1979, p. 26.
2. R. B. Beckett (ed.), *John Constable's Discourses*, Suffolk Records Society 1970, p. 71.
3. K. Barth, *Church Dogmatics* III/1, Edinburgh: T & T Clark 1958, p. 18.
4. P. Zweig, *The Heresy of Self Love*, Princeton: Princeton University Press 1980, p. 30.
5. E. Scarry, *The Body in Pain*, Oxford: Oxford University Press 1983, p. 193.
6. Scarry, *The Body in Pain*, p. 200.
7. G. Jantzen, *God's World, God's Body*, London: Darton Longman and Todd 1984; S. McFague, *Models of God: Theology for an Ecological Age*, London: SCM Press 1987.
8. R. Swinburne, *The Coherence of Theism*, Oxford: Clarendon Press 1977, pp. 104–5.
9. Jantzen, *God's World, God's Body*, p. 127.
10. Barth, *CD* II/1, Edinburgh: T & T Clark 1957, p. 476.
11. Scarry, *The Body in Pain*, p. 213.
12. *Phaedo* 65c. But see the discussion of desire in the *Phaedrus* in Ch. 4.
13. E. Rogers, *Sexuality and the Christian Body*, Oxford: Blackwell 1999, p. 240.
14. P. Brown, *The Body and Society*, London: Faber 1989, p. 394.
15. *Confessions* 10.6. I use the translation of Henry Chadwick, Oxford: World's Classics 1992.
16. K. Marx, *Economic and Philosophical Manuscripts*, Moscow: Progress 1977, p. 105.

17. *Summa Theologiae* 3.82.4.
18. V. Parnell, 'Risking Redemption', in N. Eiesland and D. Saliers (eds), *Human Disability and the Service of God*, Nashville: Abingdon 1998, p. 257.
19. Parnell, 'Risking Redemption', p. 259.
20. M. Merleau-Ponty, *The Phenomenology of Perception*, London: Routledge 1962, p. 235.
21. Cf. Aldous Huxley, *The Art of Seeing*, London: Chatto and Windus 1943, p. 19: Sensing is not the same as perceiving. The eyes and the nervous system do the sensing, the mind does the perceiving. The faculty of perceiving is related to the individual's accumulated experiences, in other words, to memory.
22. W. Ong, *The Presence of the Word*, New Haven and London: Yale University Press 1967, p. 125.
23. Ong, *Presence of the Word*, p. 163.
24. Ong, *Presence of the Word*, p. 142. Cf. Aristotle: 'It is hearing that contributes most to the growth of intelligence. For rational discourse is a cause of instruction in virtue of its being audible . . . since it is composed of words, and each word is a symbol. Accordingly, of persons destitute from birth of either sense, the blind are more intelligent than the deaf and dumb.' *Sense and Sensibilia* 1 437a10.
25. Ong, *Presence of the Word*, p. 140. It has this meaning in contrast to all the other senses. 'Sight presents surfaces . . . smell suggests presences or absences (its association with memory is commonplace . . . smell is a come or go signal . . . taste above all discriminates . . . touch . . . helps form the concepts of exteriority and interiority . . . but to explore an interior, touch must violate the interior . . . sound, on the other hand, reveals the interior without the necessity of physical invasion . . . Sound reveals interiors because its nature is determined by interior relationships.' Ong, *Presence of the Word*, pp. 117–18.
26. I. Allende, *Aphrodite*, London: Flamingo 1998, p. 105.
27. G. Steiner, 'Silence and the Poet', in *Language and Silence*, London: Faber & Faber 1967, p. 58.
28. *Laws* 2.659e.
29. *Republic* 3.402.
30. *Politics* 1337a.

31. Steiner, 'Silence and the Poet', p. 62.
32. *Timaeus* 47b.
33. *Sense and Sensibilia* 1 437a5.
34. F. Bacon, 'The Great Instauration', in J. Spedding et al. (eds), *Works*, 14 vols (1857–64), vol. 4, p. 30.
35. R. Descartes, *Discourse on Method*, in E. S. Haldane and G. Ross (eds), *Philosophical Works*, vol. 1, Cambridge: Cambridge University Press 1968, p. 104.
36. M. Jay, *Downcast Eyes: the Denigration of Vision in Twentieth Century French Thought*, Berkeley: University of California Press 1994, p. 6.
37. M. Merleau-Ponty, *Phenomenology, Language and Society*, cited in A. Synnot, *The Body Social: Symbolism, Self and Society*, London: Routledge 1993, p. 215.
38. O. von Simson, *The Gothic Cathedral*, London: Routledge & Kegan Paul 1956, pp. 49–55.
39. R. Sutcliff, *Blue Remembered Hills*, Oxford: Oxford University Press 1984, p. 132.
40. R. Paulson, *Literary Landscape: Turner and Constable*, New Haven: Yale University Press 1982, p. 49.
41. So Paulson, *Literary Landscape*, p. 80.
42. Pierre Mandrou, *Introduction to Modern France 1500–1640*, quoted by Jay, *Downcast Eyes*, p. 35. Jay is completely sceptical of the claim.
43. *On the Soul* II.9 421a21.
44. E. Dussel, *Philosophy of Liberation*, Maryknoll: Orbis 1985, p. 81.
45. A. Briggs, in K. Galloway (ed.), *Dreaming of Eden*, Glasgow: Wild Goose 1997, p. 42–3.
46. *On the Soul* II.10 422b10.
47. Allende, *Aphrodite*, p. 67.
48. J. D. Bauby, *The Diving Bell and the Butterfly*, London: Fourth Estate 1997, p. 44.
49. Ong, *Presence of the Word*, p. 5.
50. *On the Soul* II.9 421a9.
51. C. Classen, D. Howes and A. Synnot, *Aroma: The Cultural History of Smell*, London: Routledge 1994, p. 88.
52. Quoted in A. Synnot, *The Body Social: Symbolism, Self and*

Society, London: Routledge 1993, p. 186.

53. *Civilization and its Discontents*, Penguin Freud Library, vol. 12, p. 288.
54. Cited in Classen et al., *Aroma*, p. 13.
55. Synnot, *The Body Social*, p. 190.
56. Classen et al., *Aroma*, p. 73.
57. Classen et al., *Aroma*, p. 178.
58. J. Taylor, *Sermons*, 'The House of Feasting', cited in S. Schimmel, *The Seven Deadly Sins*, Oxford: Oxford University Press 1997, p. 122.
59. Ong, *Presence of the Word*, p. 172.
60. Ong, *Presence of the Word*, p. 110.

2. *The senses stilled*

1. Cited in M. Peppiatt, *Francis Bacon: Anatomy of an Enigma*, London: Phoenix 1997, p. 208.
2. A. Ecclestone, *Yes to God*, London: Darton, Longman & Todd 1975, p. 53–4.
3. N. Eiesland, *The Disabled God: Towards a Liberatory Theory of Disability*, Nashville: Abingdon 1994, p. 95.
4. R. Melville, 'The Iconoclasm of Francis Bacon', *World Review*, January 1951, quoted in Peppiatt, *Francis Bacon*, p. 145.
5. J. Berger, *Ways of Seeing*, Harmondsworth: Penguin 1972, p. 112.
6. B. Patterson, 'Redeemed Bodies: Fullness of Life', in N. Eiesland and D. Saliers (eds), *Human Disability and the Service of God*, Nashville: Abingdon 1998, p. 126.
7. Colin Barnes, 'Visual Impairment and Disability', in G. Hales (ed.), *Beyond Disability*, London: Sage 1996, p. 38.
8. S. French, 'The Disabled Role', in S. French (ed.), *On Equal Terms: Working with Disabled People*, Oxford: Butterworth Heinemann 1994, p. 53.
9. J. Morris, 'Prejudice', in French, *On Equal Terms*, p. 66.
10. Morris, 'Prejudice', p. 67.
11. F. Young, *Face to Face*, Edinburgh: T & T Clark 1990, p. 175.
12. Eiesland, *The Disabled God*, p. 83.
13. N. Mairs, *Carnal Acts*, Boston: Beacon Press 1996, p. 101.

14. French, *On Equal Terms*, p. 13. This definition is criticized by Disabled People's International because it fails to address the issues of education, employment and housing and because the concept of normality is accepted uncritically.

15. Eiesland, *The Disabled God*, p. 27.

16. J. Moltmann, 'Liberate Yourselves by Accepting One Another', in Eiesland and Saliers, *Human Disability and the Service of God*, p. 107.

17. S. Wendell, *The Rejected Body*, New York and London: Routledge 1996, p. 14.

18. Mairs, *Carnal Acts*, p. 34.

19. Young, *Face to Face*, p. 107.

20. S. Horne, ' "Those Who Are Blind See", Some New Testament Uses of Impairment, Inability and Paradox', in Eiesland and Saliers, *Human Disability and the Service of God*, p. 97.

21. Mairs, *Carnal Acts*, p. 49.

22. Contemporaries saw this as analogous to creating the world out of chaos. Paulson, *Literary Landscape*, p. 66.

23. B. Brewster, 'Access All Areas', *The Big Issue* (South West), 26 June–2 July 2000.

24. Jenny Morris, 'Prejudice', in French, *On Equal Terms*, p. 61.

25. S. French, 'Images of Disability', in French, *On Equal Terms*, p. 38.

26. French, 'Images of Disability', p. 43.

27. Eiesland, *The Disabled God*, p. 74.

28. O. Temkin, *The Double Face of Janus and Other Essays in the History of Medicine*, Baltimore and London: Johns Hopkins University Press 1977, p. 54.

29. Moltmann, 'Liberate Yourselves', p. 121.

30. Young, *Face to Face*, pp. 169, 181.

31. Mairs, *Carnal Acts*, p. 18.

32. N. Mairs, *Ordinary Time: Cycles in Marriage, Faith and Renewal*, Boston: Beacon Press 1996, pp. 17–32.

33. N. Mairs, *Plaintext*, Tucson: University of Arizona Press 1986, p. 20.

34. S. Sainsbury, *Deaf Worlds: A Study of Integration, Segregation and Disability*, London: Hutchinson 1986. The study was undertaken in two London boroughs, and in a variety of homes

and hospitals around the country: in three residential homes for the deaf, in five residential homes for the aged, in a hostel for young deaf people, and another intended to rehabilitate ex-psychiatric patients, two psychiatric hospitals and two hospitals for the mentally handicapped.

35. 'Deaf' is used to indicate profoundly deaf; 'deaf' to indicate some hearing.
36. Sainsbury, *Deaf Worlds*, pp. 10–11.
37. Sainsbury, *Deaf Worlds*, p. 102.
38. Sainsbury, *Deaf Worlds*, p. 187.
39. Sainsbury, *Deaf Worlds*, p. 84.
40. Sainsbury, *Deaf Worlds*, p. 82.
41. Sainsbury, *Deaf Worlds*, p.31.
42. Sainsbury, *Deaf Worlds*, p. 91.
43. Sainsbury, *Deaf Worlds*, pp. 296–7.
44. Nora Groce, 'Everyone Here Spoke Sign Language', in S. Gregory and G. Hartley (eds), *Constructing Deafness*, Milton Keynes: Open University 1994, p. 13.
45. P. C. Higgins, *Outsiders in a Hearing World*, London: Sage 1980, p. 101.
46. E. Goffman, *Stigma*, Harmondsworth: Penguin 1968, pp. 127–8.
47. Young, *Face to Face*, p. 22.
48. Young, *Face to Face*, p. 59.
49. Young, *Face to Face*, p. 51.
50. Young, *Face to Face*, p. 61.
51. Moltmann, 'Liberate Yourselves', p. 120.
52. Quoted in Eiesland, *The Disabled God*, p. 33.
53. Wendell, *The Rejected Body*, p. 81.
54. R. A. Scott, *The Making of Blind Men: A Study of Adult Socialization*, London and New Brunswick: Transaction 1981, p. 4.
55. S. French, 'Dimensions of Disability and Impairment', in *On Equal Terms*, p. 18.
56. Mairs, *Carnal Acts*, p. 12.
57. Mairs, *Carnal Acts*, p. 40.
58. D. Pailin, *A Gentle Touch*, London: SPCK 1992, p. 100.
59. Pailin, *A Gentle Touch*, p. 118.

60. Young, *Face to Face*, p. 109.
61. Wendell, *The Rejected Body*, p. 69.
62. Young, *Face to Face*, p. 182.
63. Horne, 'Those Who Are Blind See', p. 98.
64. Scott, *The Making of Blind Men*, p. 14.
65. Scott, *The Making of Blind Men*, p. 36.
66. Mairs, *Carnal Acts*, p. 111.
67. Mairs, *Carnal Acts*, pp. 114–15.
68. S. French, 'Disabled Health and Welfare Professionals', in *On Equal Terms*, p. 220.
69. French, 'Disabled Health and Welfare Professionals', p. 221.
70. Young, *Face to Face*, p. 179.
71. Young, *Face to Face*, p. 191.
72. Jan McLaren, 'Kathleen', in G. Horobin and D. May (eds), *Living with Mental Handicap*, London: Kingsley 1988, p. 127.
73. Wendell, *The Rejected Body*, p. 113.
74. Moltmann, 'Liberate Yourselves', p. 113.
75. Eiesland, *The Disabled God*, p. 96.
76. Moltmann, 'Liberate Yourselves', p. 111.
77. Eiesland, *The Disabled God*, p. 101.
78. Eiesland, *The Disabled God*, p. 11.
79. Moltmann, 'Liberate Yourselves', p. 116.
80. Moltmann, 'Liberate Yourselves', p. 117.
81. Pailin, *A Gentle Touch*, p. 164.
82. Young, *Face to Face*, p. 107. Aquinas argued that the most perfect stage of human development was the age of 30, which he called 'youth', between childhood and age. In relation to that he argued that 'Human beings will rise again without any defect of human nature, because as God founded human nature without a defect, even so will he restore it without defect' (*ST* 3.81.1). *Mutatis mutandis* we might apply this argument to the idea of gestalt.

3. *Sins of the flesh?*

1. M. Kahr, *Velazquez: The Art of Painting*, New York: Harper and Row 1976, p. 214.
2. Cf. E. R. Dodds, *Pagan and Christian in an Age of Anxiety*,

Cambridge: Cambridge University Press 1965, p. 35; U. Ranke-Heienemann, *Eunuchs for the Kingdom of Heaven*, Harmondsworth: Penguin 1991, *passim*.

3. P. Brown, *The Body and Society: Men, Women and Sexual Renunciation in Early Christianity*, London: Faber 1988, p. 48.

4. R. Bultmann, *Theology of the New Testament*, vol. 1, London: SCM Press 1952, p. 239.

5. R. Jewett, *Paul's Anthropological Terms*, Leiden: Brill 1971, p 114.

6. J. Moltmann, *God in Creation*, London: SCM Press 1985, p. 257.

7. T. Eagleton, *The Idea of Culture*, Oxford: Blackwell 2000, p. 99.

8. Chrysostom, *Concerning the Statues*, III.11, Nicene and Post Nicene Fathers, vol. 9, p. 359.

9. *Confessions*, 10.35.

10. N. Bryson, *Tradition and Desire: From David to Delacroix*, Cambridge: Cambridge University Press 1984, p. 209.

11. Cited in Synnot, *The Body Social*, p. 220.

12. L. Irigaray, 'Les femmes, la pornographie et l'erotisme', cited in Jay, *Downcast Eyes*, p. 493.

13. C. Itzin (ed.), *Pornography: Women, Violence and Civil Liberties*, Oxford: Oxford University Press 1992, pp. 27, 39.

14. L. Kipnis, *Bound and Gagged: Pornography and the Politics of Fantasy in America*, Durham, NC: Duke University Press 1999, p. 206.

15. Itzin, *Pornography*, pp. 66–7.

16. Itzin, *Pornography*, p. 70.

17. P. Baker, in Itzin, *Pornography*, pp. 132–3.

18. Kipnis, *Bound and Gagged*.

19. K. Millett, quoted in L. Williams, *Hard Core Power, Pleasure and the 'Frenzy of the Visible'*, London: Pandora 1989, p. 265.

20. G. Steinem, 'Erotica and Pornography: A Clear and Present Difference', *MS Magazine* (November 1978), in L. Lederer (ed.), *Take Back the Night*, New York: William Morrow 1980.

21. R. Scruton, *Sexual Desire: A Philosophical Investigation*, London: Weidenfeld & Nicolson 1986, p. 139.

22. Williams, *Hard Core*, p. 277.
23. L. Nead, *The Female Nude, Art, Obscenity and Sexuality*, London: Routledge 1992, p. 103.
24. Williams, *Hard Core*, p. 277.
25. L. Segal, 'Sweet Sorrows, Painful Pleasures', in Segal and McIntosh (eds), *Sex Exposed*, London: Virago 1992, p. 85.
26. Angela Carter, *The Sadeian Woman*, London: Virago 1979, pp. 19–20.
27. J. Berger, *Ways of Seeing*, Harmondsworth: Penguin 1972, p. 57.
28. W. Countryman, *Dirt, Greed and Sex: Sexual Ethics in the New Testament and their Implications for Today*, London: SCM Press 1989, p. 245.
29. Kipnis, *Bound and Gagged*, p. 206.
30. Brown, *Body and Society*, p. 231. Brown speaks of 'a sharpened awareness of the permanence of sexual fantasy . . . Sexual desire revealed the knot of unsurrendered privacy that lay at the very heart of fallen man. Thus, in the new language of the desert, sexuality became . . . an ideogram of the unopened heart' (p. 230).
31. This is echoed in Coleridge's famous distinction between fancy and imagination in *Biographia Litteraria* (ch. 13), where fancy lacks the truly creative power of imagination.
32. Kipnis, *Bound and Gagged*, p. 203.
33. 'The sense of pleasure and danger that violation of pollution taboos invokes in us clearly depends on the existence, within every culture, of symbolic maps or codes' (Kipnis, *Bound and Gagged*, p. 143). This recalls Paul's discussion in Romans 7 of the way in which 'law provokes us to sin'. It presumably lies behind the burgeoning genre of amateur pornography, which is presumably more about the thrill of the illicit than about self-exposure.
34. G. Steiner, 'Night Words', in *Language and Silence*, p. 98. Cf. the Williams Committee on pornography in Britain in 1979, which felt that 'Pornography crosses the line between the private and the public since it makes available in the form, for instance, of a photograph, some sexual act of a private kind and makes it available for a voyeuristic interest . . . it represents the projection into public of the private world – private, that is to

say, of the participants – of sexual activity.

35. Eagleton, *The Idea of Culture*, p. 90.
36. Steiner, *Language and Silence*, p. 73.
37. Cited in Schimmel, *Seven Deadly Sins*, p. 23.
38. G. Orwell, *The Road to Wigan Pier*, London: Gollancz 1937, p. 157.
39. Barth, *CD* IV/3, Edinburgh: T & T Clark 1961, p. 438.
40. Barth *CD* IV/3, pp. 457–9.
41. K. Barth, *Letters 1961–8*, Edinburgh: T & T Clark 1981, p. 328.
42. Barth, *CD* IV/3, p. 457.
43. Barth, *CD* IV/3, p. 451.
44. Barth, *CD* IV/3, pp. 436–7.
45. Quoted in E. Peters, *Torture*, Oxford: Blackwell 1985, p. 75.
46. Scarry, *The Body in Pain*, pp. 48–9.
47. Eagleton, *The Idea of Culture*, pp. 105, 107.
48. Peters, *Torture*, p. 179.
49. Peters, *Torture*, p. 179.
50. B. Keenan, *An Evil Cradling*, London: Vintage 1993, p. 147.
51. Keenan, *An Evil Cradling*, p. 242.
52. E. Fromm, *The Anatomy of Human Destructiveness*, Harmondsworth: Penguin 1973, p. 386.
53. W. Cavanaugh, *Torture and Eucharist*, Oxford: Blackwell 1998, p. 57.
54. Cf. Augustine, *Confessions* 10.31.
55. Kipnis, *Bound and Gagged*, ch. 3.
56. Classen et al., *Aroma*, p. 51.
57. Orwell, *The Road to Wigan Pier*, p. 159.
58. Synnot, *The Body Social*, p. 202.
59. Cited in Classen et al., *Aroma*, p. 175.
60. J. Taylor, *The House of Feasting*, in *The Sermons of the Revd J. Taylor XV–XVI*, ed. Robert Carter, London 1840, p. 110.
61. Barth, *CD* IV/2, p. 461. My italics.
62. Moltmann, *God in Creation*, p. 259.
63. G. Craig, *Germany 1866–1945*, Oxford: Oxford University Press 1978, p. 763.
64. E. Fromm, *The Art of Loving*, London: George Allen & Unwin 1962, p. 91.
65. R. Williams, 'The Body's Grace', in *Ourselves, Our Souls and*

Bodies: Sexuality and the Household of God, Boston: Cowley Publications 1996, p. 64.

4. *The education of desire*

1. Cited in B. Lewis, *Georges Grosz: Art and Politics in the Weimar Republic*, Madison: University of Wisconsin Press 1971, p. 8.
2. *Chagall on Chagall*, New York: Harrison House 1979, p. 187.
3. N. Wolf, *The Beauty Myth*, London: Vintage 1991, p. 100.
4. R. Murphy, *The Body Silent*, New York: Norton 1990, p. 114.
5. S. Miles, *Consumerism as a Way of Life*, London: Sage 1998, p. 1.
6. Miles, *Consumerism as a Way of Life*, p. 25.
7. John O'Neil, *Five Bodies*, Ithaca: Cornell University Press 1985, p. 101.
8. M. Featherstone, *Consumer Culture and Postmodernism*, London: Sage 1991, p. 91.
9. F. Fukuyama, 'Reflections on the End of History, Five Years Later', in *After History? Francis Fukuyama and His Critics*, ed. T. Burns, Lanham: Rowman and Littlefield 1994, p. 241.
10. Countryman, *Dirt, Greed and Sex*, p. 151 ff.
11. *Philebus* 66.
12. *Republic* IV 439d.
13. *Republic* IV 442a.
14. *Symposium* 211d. Catherine Pickstock argues that Plato's 'more positive' approach to physicality in the *Phaedrus*, his account of its mediating role in our knowledge of the good, 'frees him from the charge of otherworldliness and total withdrawal from physicality'. *After Writing*, Oxford: Blackwell 1998, p. 14. To be sure. The problem is that there is a profound ambivalence about the physical, and therefore about physical desire, in Plato, which fell apart in Neoplatonism, teaching Plotinus, famously, to be ashamed of being in a body. This ambivalence fed into the Christian tradition.
15. This is a prominent theme of the 'Radical Orthodoxy' group. Thus Pickstock argues that Socratic desire 'does not lack its object in the ordinary sense of lack, but attains its goal in and through its act of desiring'. *After Writing*, p. 13. Cf. also

Michael Hanby, 'Desire', in *Radical Orthodoxy*, ed. J. Milbank, C. Pickstock and G. Ward, London: Routledge 1999, pp. 109–26. The question is, of course, whether this is anything we experience other than momentarily, or whether it is primarily an eschatological or utopian reality. Since this book went to press Graham Ward's profound discussion of desire in *Cities of God* (London: Routledge 2000) has appeared, and I would recommend that discussion to any interested readers.

16. *On the Soul* 10.
17. *Rhetoric* 1 1370a1.
18. *Nicomachean Ethics* 3.11 1118a 15–25.
19. *Politics* 1. 9 1258a.
20. *Nicomachean Ethics* 1174b–1176a.
21. *Confessions* I.1.
22. Aquinas, *Summa Theologiae* 1a 2ae 26.2.
23. *ST* 1a2ae 26.4. Cf. 28.4 'In love of desire, the lover is "carried out of himself" in the sense that he is not content to enjoy what is already in his possession, but is anxious to enjoy something which is as yet outside his grasp; but since he is anxious to have that other thing for himself, he is not "carried out of himself" tout court; the ultimate term of his feeling lies within himself. In love of friendship, however, the ultimate term of the person's feeling is "located outside of him"; tout court, for he wants some good thing for his friend and works for it, exercising thought and care about his friend's interests for his friend's sake.'
24. Sebastian Moore, *Jesus the Liberator of Desire*, New York: Crossroad 1989, p. 93.
25. S. Freud, *Civilization and its Discontents*, in *Civilization, Society and Religion*, vol. 12 of the Penguin Freud Library, Harmondsworth: Penguin 1991, p. 313. Since Freud, this wider reference has tended to get lost. So, for example, Bataille's study of eroticism concentrates on the 'plethoric disorder' of the erotic instinct. Where Freud saw civilization as struggling between Eros and Thanatos, the instinct for life and the instinct for destruction, Bataille tried to understand them together. 'The violence of this disturbance reopens in the mind of the person experiencing it the abyss that death once revealed . . . secretly

and at the deepest level this disruption belongs intimately to human sensuality and is the mainspring of pleasure. In the human sphere sexual activity has broken away from animal simplicity. It is in essence a transgression, not, after the taboo, a return to primitive freedom.' G. Bataille, *Eroticism*, London: Boyars 1987, p. 104. Desire, for him, is essentially the experience of *amour fou*, the 'desire to go keeling helplessly over, that assails the innermost depths of every human being' which is the desire to 'live the limits of the possible and the impossible with ever increasing intensity.' Bataille, *Eroticism*, p. 239. This is more or less exactly how the Gnostics understood eroticism, according to Peter Brown. In Gnosticism, he says, 'Sexual desire was made to stand out in sharp relief as an enduring feature of the unredeemed person: it stood for the headlong energy of a universe that was opposed to the cool tranquillity of the realm of the unmoving spirit. Those who indulge in sexual passion 'show that they are assisting the world'. Brown, *The Body and Society*, p. 116.

26. G. Deleuze and F. Guattari, *Anti Oedipus*, London: Athlone 1984, p. 347.

27. B. Turner, *The Body and Society*, 2nd edn, London: Sage 1996, p. 57. The distinction between needs and desires is anticipated by Aristotle's distinction between worthy and less worthy pleasures. Aquinas comments: 'a thing may be pleasurable in two ways. First it may appeal to the very nature of an animal, as do food, drink and the like; desire of that sort of pleasurable object is called "natural" desire. Second, a thing may be pleasurable because an animal perceives it under some special aspect which makes it seem appealing; for when one sees a thing as good and appealing, one consequently takes pleasure in it. Desire of pleasurable things of that kind is called "non-natural", and in Latin the word *cupiditas* is usually reserved for it' (*ST* 1a2ae 30.3).

28. E. P. Thompson, *William Morris: Romantic to Revolutionary*, London: Phaedon 1976, pp. 786–7, my italics.

29. S. Freud, *Beyond the Pleasure Principle*, tr. J. Strachey, London: Hogarth 1950, p. 56.

30. Fromm, *The Art of Loving*, pp. 62–3.

31. N. Postman, *Amusing Ourselves to Death*, London: Methuen 1987, pp. 161, 168.

32. R. Bahro, *Avoiding Social and Ecological Disaster*, Bath: Gateway 1994, p. 145.

33. Bahro, *Avoiding Social and Ecological Disaster*, p. 109.

34. A. T. Durning, *How Much is Enough*, London: Earthscan 1992, p. 107.

35. Bahro, *Avoiding Social and Ecological Disaster*, p. 220.

36. Bahro, *Avoiding Social and Ecological Disaster*, p. 25.

37. Bahro, *Avoiding Social and Ecological Disaster*, p. 219.

38. Bahro, *Avoiding Social and Ecological Disaster*, pp. 108, 158.

39. B. Wielenga, *Towards an Eco Just Society*, Bangalore: CSA 1999, p. 136.

40. K. Galloway (ed.), *Dreaming of Eden*, Glasgow: Wild Goose 1997, p. 113.

41. Brown, *The Body and Society*, pp. 426–7. He goes on: 'The Christian married couple must "descend with a certain sadness" to intercourse: for in the act their very bodies spoke to them of Adam's fall. In Augustine's piercing vision the city and the house were washed by a dark current of sexual shame. Adam's shame knew no frontiers. All men and women must feel it.'

42. Brown, *The Body and Society*, p. 235.

43. N. Mairs, *Remembering the Bone House*, Boston: Beacon 1989, p. 173.

44. Cyprian, *de habitu virginum* 1, cited in Brown, *The Body and Society*, p. 193.

45. Brown, *The Body and Society*, p. 226.

46. Brown, *The Body and Society*, p. 60.

47. In *Larkrise to Candleford*, Flora Thompson describes peasant life in England in the 1880s as a 'generation under siege'.

48. Wielenga, *Towards an Eco Just Society*, p. 148.

49. D. Korten, *The Post Corporate World*, Connecticut: Kumarian 2000, p. 219.

50. Bahro, *Avoiding Social and Ecological Disaster*, p. 73.

51. Conrad Lodziak challenges the idea of an alternative education, arguing that what we need is far more autonomy. I am hesitant about the term autonomy because of its centrality to the Enlightenment project of human beings without God, human

beings supposedly come of age. At the same time it seems to me that what he means by autonomy is what the Christian tradition has meant by the disciplined believer. C. Lodziak, *Manipulating Needs: Capitalism and Culture*, London: Pluto 1995, ch. 3.

52. Countryman, *Dirt, Greed and Sex*, p. 267.
53. Bahro, *Avoiding Social and Ecological Disaster*, p. 233.
54. Bahro, *Avoiding Social and Ecological Disaster*, p. 262.
55. Bahro, *Avoiding Social and Ecological Disaster*, p. 103.
56. Wielenga, *Towards an Eco Just Society*, p. 163.

5. *Celebrating bodies*

1. Bahro, *Avoiding Social and Ecological Disaster*, p. 228.
2. V. Parnell, 'Risking Redemption', in Eiesland and Saliers, *Human Disability and the Service of God*, p. 251.
3. Parnell, 'Risking Redemption', p. 264.
4. The 1999 film by Wim Wenders about a group of musicians in Havana.
5. Quoted in V. Shiva, *Biopiracy*, Totnes: Green Books 1998, p. 42.
6. B. Kneen, *Farmageddon*, Gabriola, Canada: New Society 1999, p. 29.
7. W. Cavanaugh, *Torture and Eucharist*, Oxford: Blackwell 1999, p. 58.

Suggestions for Further Reading

I. Allende, *Aphrodite*, London: Flamingo 1998

Aristotle, *Collected Works*, ed. J. Barnes, Princeton: Princeton University Press 1984

J. D. Bauby, *The Diving Bell and the Butterfly*, London: Fourth Estate 1997

P. Brown, *The Body and Society*, London: Faber & Faber 1989

C. Classen, D. Howes and A. Synnot, *Aroma: The Cultural History of Smell*, London: Routledge 1994

E. Dussel, *Philosophy of Liberation*, Maryknoll: Orbis 1985

N. Eiesland and D. Saliers (eds), *Human Disability and the Service of God*, Nashville: Abingdon 1998

K. Galloway (ed.), *Dreaming of Eden*, Glasgow: Wild Goose 1997

G. Jantzen, *God's World, God's Body*, London: Darton, Longman and Todd 1984

M. Jay, *Downcast Eyes: the Denigration of Vision in Twentieth Century French Thought*, Berkeley: University of California Press 1994

S. McFague, *Models of God: Theology for an Ecological Age*, London: SCM Press 1987

M. Merleau-Ponty, *The Phenomenology of Perception*, London: Routledge 1962

W. Ong, *The Presence of the Word*, New Haven and London: Yale University Press 1967

Plato, *The Collected Dialogues*, ed. E. Hamilton and H. Cairns, Princeton: Princeton University Press 1961

E. Rogers, *Sexuality and the Christian Body*, Oxford: Blackwell 1999

Suggestions for Further Reading

E. Scarry, *The Body in Pain*, Oxford: Oxford University Press 1983

S. Schimmel, *The Seven Deadly Sins*, Oxford: Oxford University Press 1997

G. Steiner, *Language and Silence*, London: Faber & Faber 1967

A. Synnot, *The Body Social: Symbolism, Self and Society*, London: Routledge 1993

Index

Index

Index